Palestinian Cultures
of Resistance

Mahmood Darwash / Fadwa Tuqan / Ghassan Kanafani / Naj al-Ali

Michael Lavalette

a Redwords book

REDWORDS

Palestinian Cultures of Resistance:
Mahmood Darwash / Fadwa Tuqan / Ghassan Kanafani / Naj al-Ali
By Michael Lavalette
Published by Redwords June 2021

Design and production: Roger Huddle
Set in 9.5/12 Janson text
Printed by Halstan Press, Amersham HP6 6HJ

Redwords is linked to Bookmarks the Socialist Bookshop
1 Bloomsbury Street, London WC1B 3QE

https://bookmarksbookshop.co.uk

ISBN: 978-1-912926-01-5

The author: Michael Lavalette is Professor of Social Work at Liverpool Hope University. He has visited Palestine on numerous occasions, leading regular solidarity visits for students and activists to refugee camps across the West Bank. He was a socialist councillor in Preston (2004-2015) during which time he led a campaign to twin Preston with Nablus and, during an Israeli assault on Gaza, fly the Palestinian flag over the town hall. His previous writings on Palestine include the book Voice from the West Bank, written with Chris Jones and published by Bookmarks in 2011.

Contents

6

Achnowledgements

THIS BOOK DEVELOPED out of a discussion I had with some colleagues on a field trip to Palestine in 2018. Thanks to Steve Lucas and Tracy Ramsey for engaging with the idea and pushing me to give it a go! Dave Gilchrist at Bookmarks and Roger Huddle at Redwords both thought the idea worth pursuing and their support has been invaluable. Roger deserves particular thanks for his patience as I missed (several) writing deadlines, as first the UCU strike and then the Covid-19 pandemic (and helping to coordinate the Social Work Action Network response), got in the way of completing the book.

In Palestine I was greatly helped by the staff, and librarians in particular, at the Alistiqlal University in Jericho, where one of the sections is named after Ghassan Kanafani. Thanks are due to the head of the board of trustees Gen. Dr Tawfiq Terawi for his help and support.

I was honoured to meet and interview a number of cultural figures in Palestine in March 2019. Thanks, for their time and insight, to former Undersecretary for Cultural Affairs in the Palestinian Authority Mutawakel Taha, Nafeth Alrefa'i, general secretary of the Palestinian Writers Union, Shehab Hammed, deputy chair of the Palestinian Writers Union, Nassar Ibrahimi, Dr Mohamed Farhat and Faris Saban'I at the Darwish museum.

I would like to thank Liverpool Hope University for funding several trips to Palestine over the years and for their consistent support for my research in this field. They have also been incredibly supportive of the regular student field trips I organize to the West Bank. The University regularly receives letters and emails complaining about my work in Palestine. They have been unswerving in their support for the research and the rights of academic freedom of speech and research.

Thanks, as always, to Laura Penketh, for 'holding the fort' as I disappeared off to Palestine (once more) and for reading and commenting on draft chapters. My friends and comrades Iain Ferguson, Judith Orr, John Molyneux, Chris Jones, Lindsey German, Chris Nineham, Tracy Ramsey, Steve Lucas, Vasilios Ioakimidis, Mike Morris, Mohammed Amara and Naela Abu Tahoun all read and commented on drafts. The manuscript is better for their input; of course, responsibility for what is written rests with me.

Finally, this book would simply not have been possible without the support and friendship of the Amara family in Tulkarem. Over the years the family have taken me and various student groups into their homes and patiently explained life in the camps to us.

I first met Mohammed Amara in 2004 when I organised a delegation from Preston to the West Bank. I had been elected as a socialist councillor the previous year and had attempted (unsuccessfully) to twin Preston with Nablus. We may have lost the vote but the campaign helped to raise Palestinian solidarity in the city to great heights. In the years that followed, we had some massive demonstrations, fundraising events and meetings in the city.

Out of the twinning campaign came an invite from the Palestinian Authority to travel to the West Bank. We went during the Second Intifada. That was when I first met Mohammed. He managed to manoeuvre 34 of us around the West Bank, avoiding, for the most part, contact with and disruption from Israeli occupation forces. He also arranged for us to meet with President Arafat. We would come to realise that we were the last international delegation to meet him before his untimely death.

In the years that followed, Mohammed and I became close friends—'brothers in the struggle', as he puts it. Mohammed facilitated the research I did with Chris Jones which led to the book Voices from the West Bank (Bookmarks, 2010). More recently he has worked with me to organise the bi-annual student field trips to the West Bank that we run from Liverpool Hope University.

Mohammed and Naela (and Manal, Omar, Samar and Ibraheim) open their home to me, feed me, look after me and work tirelessly to support our students and our research. I would like to dedicate this book to them, with heartfelt thanks, for everything they do.

9

For Mohammed Amara and Naela Abu Tahoun
Thawra hatta al nas'r

A note on terminology.

In what follows I use the term Palestine48 to refer to the areas of Palestine that were taken by Israel in the war of 1948. The West Bank refers to the part of Palestine that was held by Jordan after the 1948 war, more than the present cantonized areas under Palestinian Authority control. When I refer to the troops of the IDF, I refer to them as Israeli soldiers or troops. I use Jerusalem/AlQuds to give the city both its recognized Western name and its Arab name.

Introduction
'Rocks in the valley'

IN THIS BOOK I LOOK at the lives and work of four great Palestinian cultural figures: Ghassan Kanafani (1936-1972), Mahmoud Darwish (1941-2008), Fadwa Tuqan (1917-2003) and Naji al-Ali (1936-1987).

Together they are exponents of what is sometimes termed 'classical Palestinian national-resistance art'. Their work is symbolic of a period when "Palestinian art became more systematically a platform for the nationalist resistance movement" (Salih & Richter-Devroe, 2014: p9). Emotionally and culturally, their art gave voice to the Palestinian people's aspirations for freedom. It depicts the trauma of refugee life and exile, the horrors of occupation and brutal oppression, and it celebrates the heroism of resistance.

The high point of national resistance art ran between the late 1960s and the 1990s. These dates coincided with the rise to dominance of Fatah within the Palestine Liberation Organisation (PLO). The period covers the PLO's adoption of the strategy of 'revolutionary war' for liberation up until the signing of the Oslo Accords and the subsequent establishment of the Palestinian Authority (PA).

After it was established, the PA had a contradictory role in relation to cultural production. On the one hand it became a sponsor of resistance culture. On the other, it attempted to normalize relations with both the occupying power and global imperialism. Some characterized the role of the PA as a 'subcontractor' or 'enforcer' of Israeli authority, who played a key role in repressing and preventing "Palestinian resistance against Israeli oppression" (Kayali, 2021: p2). Culturally, one of the consequences was that formal national resistance art increasingly became a stale and crude caricature of what it had once been.

But the work of Kanafani, Darwish, Tuqan and al-Ali represents the high point of Palestinian national resistance art. Their cultural production was always deeply affected by their direct experiences. All four had been subject to colonial occupation, under the British Mandate, the Nakba, the Palestinian term meaning the disaster or catastrophe of the ethnic cleansing that took place in 1947/8, of settler-colonialism—the establishment of the state of Israel, created in 1948—and of the Naksa of 1967, which saw Israel emerge victorious from the Six-Day War in June and take control of the West Bank, Gaza and East Jerusalem (from the Jordanians), the Golan Heights (from Syria) and the Sinai Peninsula (from Egypt).

Darwish, Kanafani and al-Ali lived through displacement as refugees. Tuqan was a resident of Nablus on the West Bank, which, during the Nakba, came under Jordanian control and was then captured by the Israelis in the Naksa of 1967.

Ghassan Kanafani was born in Acre, on Palestine's northern Mediterranean coast, in 1936. During the Nakba his family were forced to flee. They eventually ended up settling in Syria's capital Damascus.

Kanafani was a journalist, an editor, a novelist, a playwright, an artist and a political and literary theorist. During his life, he published three novels, a play and more than 50 short stories, as well as numerous articles for newspapers and journals.

His novels were amongst the first to focus on the plight of Palestinian refugees. His works of literary theory were significant because they drew attention to a number of Arab writers inside Palestine48. He was important in bringing the poetry of Mahmoud Darwish to the wider diaspora.

His artistic talents were put to use by the Popular Front for the Liberation of Palestine (PFLP) as he designed their distinctive

Ghassan Kanafani

Leila Khaled

logo—with the white arrow pointing the route of return to Palestine48.

But Kanafani was also an activist. In the early 1950s whilst at University, he joined the Arab Nationalist Movement and encountered George Habash. He would later move to join the PFLP, founded in 1967 by Habash. The PFLP would soon become the second largest group within the Palestinian Liberation Organisation (PLO) umbrella.

The PFLP identifies itself as a revolutionary Marxist party—its political orientation drawn from Maoist and Guevarist traditions of armed struggle for national liberation. Perhaps the PFLP's most famous member was (and is) Leila Khaled, the "icon of Palestinian liberation" (Irving, 2012), whose image, with a keffiyeh on her head and an AK47 in her hands, has been reproduced across the globe—and can be seen today on the Apartheid Wall at the Bethlehem checkpoint.

Kanafani was martyred by a car-bomb planted by Mossad agents on 8 July 1972.

Mahmoud Darwish was born in the village of Birweh in the Western Galilee, in 1942. He lived there with his family until they were forcibly expelled in 1948. Initially they fled to Lebanon but soon returned to set up home in the Palestinian village of al-Jadeeda in Palestine.

Darwish and his family lived in Lebanon for twelve months after their displacement, and during that time Israel conducted its first census. Because they were in Lebanon, they were not counted as Arab Israelis, but because the family returned, they were never formally identified as refugees either, becoming part

13

of the 'internally displaced'. The Israelis referred to his status, and those in similar positions, as a 'present-absentee alien'.

He attended a local Arab school, but his teachers had to hide him anytime there was a school inspection because he did not have citizen status. He grew up immersed in the stories of the Quran, the Bible and the Torah, and would later use biblical figures in his poetry. He read Hebrew partly because there was a clamp down on Arabic publications within Palestine48 and partly because his generation had to be able to read in Hebrew to access literature. When he left school, he was barred from attending university because of his 'non-status'.

Darwish joined the Israeli Communist Party, where he worked alongside people from all community backgrounds, and many of his friends and comrades were Jewish. He began to publish poems in Arabic in the Communist press and to recite them to large audiences. As a result, he often found himself in prison.

It is this background that helps explain both his hostility to Zionism and the Israeli state, but also his opposition to antisemitism. In the biographical documentary made by French director Simone Bitton (1997), he makes the following point:

> The military judge who punished me for my poetry was Jewish. The woman teacher who taught me Hebrew, and inspired my love of literature, was Jewish. The English teacher, a stern man, was Jewish. The woman judge who presided over my first trial was Jewish. My first lover was Jewish. My next-door neighbour was Jewish, and my political comrades were Jewish. Therefore, I did not look at Jews as a separate entity, I did not have a stereotyped view. Thus, from the beginning, for me, coexistence has seemed possible psychologically and culturally. But the main problem remains the political one.

Darwish left Palestine48 to study in the Soviet Union in 1970, and from there he moved first to Egypt and then to Lebanon. He joined the PLO in 1973, at which point he was banned from re-entering Palestine48. In 1988 he wrote the Palestinian Declaration

Fadwa Tuqan

Naji al-Ali

of Independence but, in 1993, resigned from the PLO Executive Committee after the PLO signed the Oslo Accords.

His life in exile included time living across the Arab world in Cairo, Beirut, Tunis, Amman and Ramallah. When he died of heart failure in 2008, the Palestinian Authority announced three days of mourning and thousands attended his funeral.

He is recognised as Palestine's national poet. There is a large museum and cultural centre dedicated to him and his life in Ramallah (which is well worth visiting alongside the Palestinian National Museum, also in Ramallah, if you ever travel to the West Bank).

During his lifetime, Darwish published over 30 volumes of poetry and eight books of prose.

Fadwa Tuqan was in born in 1917 and for most of her life she lived in the West Bank city of Nablus. Nablus is a rebellious city and prides itself on its nickname 'Jabal an-Nar', which means the 'mountain of fire'. Tuqan was born into a Palestinian middle-class family in a conservative city where, in the most part, women were restricted from engagement in the male public world of education, politics, public affairs and the arts.

Her love of poetry and her developing skill as a poet were nurtured by her elder brother, the famous poet Ibrahim Tuqan. Fadwa fought for women's voices to be heard and her poetry to be taken seriously. But, particularly after the War of 1967 when Israel directly occupied the West Bank, hers became a voice of protest and anger at the reality of occupation and the threat to Palestinian society and culture.

15

Her poetry became a voice for Palestinian resistance. So much so that Israeli Defence Minister Moshe Dayan is said to have claimed that every time she wrote a poem another ten Palestinians joined the armed resistance. Tuqan died in 2003 during the Second Intifada. One of her last poems raged against the lockdown of Nablus (in 2002), which saw the city subjected to curfew for 72 days.

Naji al-Ali was born in the village of al-Shajara, in the Galilee in either 1936 or 1937. In 1948 his family were forced into exile and eventually settled in the Ain al-Hilweh refugee camp in southern Lebanon. Brought up in desperate poverty, al-Ali joined the fight for refugee rights, often ending up in (a Lebanese) prison after a protest. It was whilst in prison that he began to draw political cartoons. These cartoons brought him to the attention of Ghassan Kanafani and, through him, to the world.

Al-Ali never forgot his refugee roots. His cartoons are not only scathing in their attacks on the Israelis and their brutality towards the Palestinians but also lampoon the global imperial powers who support Israel, the Arab leaders who turn a blind eye to Palestinian suffering, and those who are often too keen to enter into agreements with their oppressors.

Al-Ali's trenchant criticism of Arab and Palestinian leaders meant he was not always popular with Palestinian politicians but he was always popular amongst the Palestinian masses. Today it is difficult to travel anywhere in the West Bank or Gaza without seeing a version of al-Ali's greatest creation: the young, ragged, Palestinian refugee Handala.

Al-Ali was murdered in London on 22 July, 1987, when a lone assassin shot him through the head. He had made enemies amongst some powerful elites across the Middle East and although some have suggested they could have been responsible for his death, evidence points to the Israelis, making al-Ali another Palestinian martyr.

There are, of course, many other great Palestinian cultural figures this book could have looked at. People like the novelists of the Diaspora Jabra Ibrahim Jabra and Samira Azzam, Palestinian writers from within Palestine48 such as Mohammad Nafta' or Mohammad 'Ali Taha, whose medium is the short story, or the poets Kamal Nasir, murdered by the Israelis in 1973, and Mourid Barghouti. But limitations of space have meant I focus on Kanafani, Darwish, Tuqan and al-Ali.

All four of my subjects are great artists in their own right and it is on these terms that they are judged. But their works also give voice to the aspirations of the Palestinian people and to the trauma experienced by refugees.

Darwish, Kanafani, Tuqan and al-Ali are also deeply entrenched within Palestinian national culture. They are widely known and revered (in a way that poets, authors and cartoonists in Britain rarely are). They have streets named after them. They are spoken about with pride, as representatives of the nation. Their names and their cultural outputs are embedded within popular consciousness. They were, and remain, identifiable cultural figures and part of the popular, national liberation movement. Today, they are viewed as a recognisable part of the resistance and are spoken about with pride across Palestinian society.

However, their importance is also reflected in the fact that although their work is rooted in the Palestinian experience, they move beyond Palestinian specificities and speak to the oppressed everywhere, reinforcing our common humanity.

For example, Kanafani's great novella *Men in the Sun* speaks directly of the Palestinian refugee experience but in doing so, highlights the common experiences of all refugees struggling to make a better life for themselves and their families in different countries, the horrors of refugee transportation routes, and the tragic deaths of refugees as they flee for their lives. In this sense, it has an important contemporary relevance. It speaks to the experience of Syrian, Afghani, Iraqi and other refugees who are fleeing war, poverty and crisis and who are today taking their lives in their hands as they try to navigate the Mediterranean or the English Channel.

The cartoons of al-Ali and his character Handala continue to speak to and on behalf of the poor and oppressed across the

Middle East and North Africa. Handala, with his back turned to the horrors and pain of the world, often with his right armed raised, sometimes in a fist, sometimes carrying a flag, sometimes carrying a pen, and sometimes an AK47, continues to grace the walls and placards of those fighting injustices across the region. Handala represents the poor whose enemies continue to be the imperialist powers, the Zionists and the Arab ruling classes.

We will explore Darwish's famous poem 'Bitaqat hawiyah' (Identity Card) in more detail later. This poem, steeped in Palestinian realities, was his most popular across the Arab world. Each verse starts with the assertion:

Write it down!
I am an Arab.

This reflects both a demand and an act of defiance against Israeli state authorities. Darwish wrote it after being arrested at a public reading of his poems. After his arrest, he was instructed to report weekly to a police station and provide his identity card details.

But the poem's popularity across the region in the 1960s and 1970s was its apparent affirmation of a more assertive Arab identity, its positive cry of defiance in the face of imperial intervention and its recognition of the necessity of anti-imperialist resistance. These themes are caught in the poem's conclusion:

Write it down!
I am an Arab
You have stolen my ancestors' orchards,
the land I farmed
with my children.
You left us nothing
except for these rocks.
Will your State take them too
as it's been said?!
So Now!
Record at the top of the first page:

I do not hate people
nor do I steal.
But if I become hungry
I will eat my robber's flesh.
Beware then, beware of my hunger
and my anger.

Tuqan's poem 'Hamza' talks of the heroic steadfastness (what the Palestinians call samoud) of 'ordinary' Palestinians and ordinary people in the face of oppression. Across the globe, the oppressors, the exploiters and the ruling classes have the full force of state power, courts, police and armed forces behind them to defend and protect their interests. 'Logically' they should win; 'logically' we should lose. But social struggles are not solved logically on paper—and Hamza-the-ordinary encapsulates this.

Hamza was just an ordinary man
like others in my hometown
who work only with their hands for bread.
When I met him the other day,
this land was wearing a cloak of mourning
in windless silence. And I felt defeated.
But Hamza-the-ordinary said:
'My sister, our land has a throbbing heart,
it doesn't cease to beat, and it endures
the unendurable. It keeps the secrets
of hills and wombs. This land sprouting
with spikes and palms is also the land
that gives birth to a freedom-fighter.

The poem continues to tell Hamza's story. The arrest of his son, the order to evacuate and destroy his home and Hamza's defiant response:

Hamza opened the window.
Face to face with the sun blazing outside,
he cried: 'in this house my children
and I will live and die
for Palestine'

One hour later the house is blown up "burying dreams and memories of a lifetime of labour, tears and some happy moments". And then the final sentences:

Yesterday I saw Hamza
walking down a street in our town—Hamza the ordinary
man
as he always was:
always secure in his determination.

Hamza's optimism and faith in a better future, his determination to fight on whatever the personal consequences are not just restricted to Palestinian realities. Hamza's is the fortitude of those who struggle for justice and the vision of a better world across the globe.

Kanafani, Darwish, Tuqan and al-Ali capture within their work a broader vision of freedom and liberation, one that speaks to the oppressed everywhere. They turn a local tragedy into a universal one; they make Palestinian issues global issues. They help bring the plight of Palestine to the world and help make Palestine an international question.

When planning this book, I interviewed Motwakel Taha, former Undersecretary of Cultural Affairs in the Palestinian Authority. He described the four as "our rocks in the valley". The phrase, drawing on an old Palestinian saying, indicates the four's importance, their stability and their rootedness. In a fast-moving world full of conflict, oppression and dispossession, the four hold on to Palestinian humanity, agency and nationhood, to refugee rights and to the prospect of a secular Palestinian society based on justice and equality for all.

The chapters that follow are primarily devoted to these four great cultural figures. However, the first chapter is more general. It attempts to do two things: to provide a historical context to the creation of the state of Israel and the expulsion of the Palestinians and, secondly, to look at the development of 'committed literature' within the Palestinian resistance movement. It may be that some readers are already familiar with this story and may wish to move directly to chapter 2.

Chapter 1
The committed artists and their context

KANAFANI, DARWISH, TUQAN and AL-ALI were born into British
Mandate Palestine. Their lives and their art developed against the
backdrop of the realities and the costs of imperial intervention in
the region and the impact of Settler-colonisation on the lives of
the indigenous Arab peoples of Palestine. This chapter provides
the background to the carve up of the Middle East region and
how this, in turn, created the space for an engaged, committed,
'resistance' literature to develop.

The present-day Middle East was created by imperial
interventions throughout the twentieth century. During the
First World War, the British government was involved in three
sets of agreements, treaties and commitments that would shape
the region.

One British war aim was to extend and deepen its Empire
across the 'Near East', as it was called at the time, and there
were two primary drivers.

First, the region had a plentiful supply of the increasingly
important commodity, oil. The importance of oil is evident
when considering that British imports of oil products increased
eleven-fold between 1900 and 1920 (Regan, 2017: p4). The first
oil field in the region was discovered in 1908 in present day Iran.

Second, the area was strategically important in linking Britain
(and other European powers, especially France) to India and
China. The opening of the Suez Canal in 1869 cut sailing times
from Britain to India and France to what was then called Indo-
China dramatically. It also encouraged imperial intervention

into East Africa and the Arabian Peninsula. As a result, the ports of Beirut, Haifa and Port Said grew in economic and strategic importance.

The (Turkish) Ottoman Empire entered the First World War on the side of Germany. The British tried to foment rebellion in the region to undermine the Turkish war effort. They entered into various agreements with different groups, making vague promises about the future shape of the Middle East should Britain and its allies win the war.

The first significant intervention came about via correspondence between the British and various Arab groups in a series of papers and letters known as the McMahon-Husayn Correspondence of 1915/16, in which the British actively encouraged Arab hopes for independence (Hourani, 1991).

In the immediate pre-war period, there was considerable agitation for greater Arab autonomy within the Ottoman empire, especially in what was known as the 'fertile crescent' (broadly the Eastern Mediterranean coast and the rivers and valleys of the Nile, Jordan, Euphrates and Tigris—present day Northern Egypt, Palestine, Lebanon, Jordan, Syria and Iraq).

The 'Young Turk' revolt of 1908 against the Sultan brought the promise of greater autonomy for the Arab provinces and greater acceptance of Turkish-Arab equality (Sorby, 2005). But the dreams were soon squashed. A demand for Syrian self-government was rejected in early 1909 and the Young Turks turned towards a process of 'Turkification' across the old Ottoman Empire. The actions of the Young Turks fuelled Arab nationalism—and it was this that the British played upon and exploited during the war.

In 1916, Husayn "the sharif of Mecca...came out in revolt against the Ottoman sultan...[and] an Arab force...fought alongside the allied forces in the occupation of Palestine and Syria" (Hourani, 1991: p316). As Mir notes:

> The Arab masses were mobilised by Sharif Hussein of Mecca to fight alongside the Allies. The Arab people...had hoped to gain independence and establish a unified Greater Syria (that included Palestine) under the Sharif. (Mir, 2013: p. 112)

Part of this story has been mythologised in the tale of 'Lawrence of Arabia'.

Whilst the specific details of any firm agreement are not clear, there was an apparent recognition by the British and its allies that those that spoke Arabic constituted a 'nation'.

In the immediate post-war period, US President Woodrow Wilson talked of the world being remade on the basis of the 'self-determination' of national entities, and the new revolutionary Soviet government in Russia was actively promoting the right of nations to self-determination. Together, these fed growing Arab demands for independence.

Yet demands for independence came up against the second British policy perspective, encapsulated in the Sykes-Picot Agreement of 1916 (Barr, 2011). Signed by the French and the British, it detailed how they would divide the Middle East in the event of an Allied victory. The details were first made public by Leon Trotsky in *Izvestia* after the Russian Revolution in late November 1917 as he determined to expose the imperial carve up of the region (Regan, 2017: p37).

The Agreement identified zones of permanent influence, with the French and British taking control of Arab resources, including oil.

Whilst the zones do not easily match contemporary countries, essentially the whole of the Middle East was to be divided into five zones (A to E). In Zone A (covering today's Lebanon, northern Syria, Kurdistan and part of Turkey), France was to establish whatever administration and control it wished. Zone B (the main part of contemporary Syria and North West Iraq) was to be an 'independent' Arab state or confederation, but France was to supply advisers and officials. Zone C was Palestine and West Jordan and was to be administered by the British (apart from Jerusalem, which was to be under international control). Zone D (the rest of Jordan and northern Saudi Arabia) were to be 'independent' Arab states, but Britain was to supply advisers and officials. Finally, Zone E (the main part of Iraq and Kuwait) was to be under direct British control (Barr, 2012).

Palestinian resources were not central to the British empire, but the port of Haifa was. British control of Haifa would allow the export of oil from the Middle East out through the Mediterranean and, at the same time, offer a port for the British fleet to re-fuel, using the Suez Canal to get to and from India (the imperial 'jewel in the crown'). Beirut, just up the Mediterranean coast, would perform a similar role for the French.

The Agreement affirms how important the region was to the imperial powers both economically and geo-politically. For both the British and the French, any form of Arab independence would need to be compatible with their over-arching imperial interests.

The third intervention, the one with the greatest ramifications for Palestine, was the Balfour Agreement of 1917.

It is important to have some understanding of the background to the Balfour Declaration. Its roots were in the Zionist movement's attempts to court the major powers at the end of the nineteenth and beginning of the twentieth centuries, combined with the interests of British imperialism in the Middle East.

Zionism is a political philosophy of Jewish nationalism. It combines partly religious and partly historical ideas that claim the world's Jewish population has a right to that part of the modern Middle East that has been home to Palestinian Arabs (Muslims, Christians and Jews) for thousands of years.

Zionist ideas only started to gain influence in Jewish communities towards the end of the nineteenth century. At this time somewhere in the region of 90 percent of the Jewish population in the world lived in Europe—and they had made important contributions to European culture in politics, the arts, literature and science.

But in Eastern Europe, in the last vestiges of European feudal societies, local rulers tried to maintain their power by deploying anti-Jewish pogroms and expelling local Jewish communities. In the last quarter of the nineteenth century, waves of deadly pogroms were launched against Eastern European Jewish communities in what was known as the Pale of Permanent Jewish

Settlement (covering parts of present-day Poland, Ukraine, Belarus and Russia) (Popoff, 2019: p10).

In the face of increasing levels of violence and oppression, the Jews of Eastern Europe began to migrate.

> From 1881 to 1914, more than 2.5 million Jews migrated from Eastern Europe, i.e. some 80,000 each year. Of these, some two million reached the United States, some 300,000 went to other overseas countries (including Palestine), while approximately 350,000 chose Western Europe.
> (Ben-Sasson, 1985)

In Western Europe, in countries such as Germany, France and Britain, poor Jewish migrants were once again faced with levels of racism.

In opposition to the rising levels of antisemitism, Jewish communities began to develop and adopt strong traditions of anarchism and socialism. The most significant Jewish organization to emerge from the Pale was the General Jewish Labour Bund (known simply as the Bund), formed in the late 1890s. The Bund was a secular socialist organization that actively campaigned against antisemitism, defended Jewish civil and cultural rights and rejected assimilation. In general terms, the Bund rejected working with religious, Zionist and conservative groups in the Jewish community and instead developed links with other socialist, labour and trade union organisations (Frankel, 1984).

But antisemitism also led to the growth of Zionism.

The architect of modern Zionism was Theodor Herzl. Herzl was a journalist who covered the trial of Albert Dreyfus, a Jewish Officer in the French army. Dreyfus faced trumped up charges of communicating French military secrets to Germany. The trial provoked an outburst of antisemitism across France. This had a profound impact on Hertzl, who concluded that the only viable solution to antisemitism was for Jews to withdraw from Europe altogether and establish their own homeland.

Hertzl was not particularly religious, but he soon identified two key elements that were to shape modern Zionism.

First, he acknowledged that Jewish biblical myths were an important source for developing an exclusivist and nationalistic Jewish identity. Thus Palestine, as the ancient homeland of the Jewish Diaspora, became the place to form the Jewish state.

Second, he deliberately linked the Zionist project to the broader European imperial scheme: he realised that to establish an exclusivist Jewish state, Zionism would need to ingratiate itself to Europe's imperial powers. Here he courted the British because they were the most significant imperial power of the age. He believed that a Jewish homeland could only be obtained by 'assured supremacy'—that is, becoming a Colonial-Settler State tied to imperial interests.

> England with her possessions in Asia should be most interested in Zionism, for the shortest route to India is by way of Palestine. England's great politicians were the first to recognise the need for colonial expansion... And so I believe in England the idea of Zionism, which is a colonial idea, should be easily understood. (Herzl, quoted in Rose, 1986: p36)

Zionist leader and future President of Israel Chaim Weizmann would play a key role in obtaining British support for the Zionist project. Weizmann was born in present-day Belarus but moved to Western Europe at the turn of the century. He lived in Manchester from 1904 and was introduced to (then Prime Minister) Arthur Balfour in 1905. In 1916 Balfour became foreign secretary in Lloyd George's coalition government.

In 1917 Weizmann was invited to secret discussions with the British government which led to the Balfour Declaration. The Declaration is short, but makes its position clear:

> His Majesty's Government views with favour the establishment in Palestine of a national home for the Jewish people, and will use their best endeavours to facilitate the achievement of this object.

The Declaration was "motivated by [British]...self-interest that coalesced with the ambitions of the Zionist movement."

For the British, the aim was to:

> Integrate this project [ie of establishing a Jewish Homeland in Palestine] into the goal of sustaining empire without appearing to replicate imperialist expansionism and colonisation. They hoped that Zionist settlement would provide a convenient surrogate, effectively implementing colonisation under the guise of national reconstruction. Zionism...became an important adjunct of British imperial strategy in the Near East. (Regan, 2017: p9)

As the First World War drew to a close, the Sykes-Picot Agreement and the Balfour Declaration were central to establishing British imperial support for a 'Jewish homeland' in Palestine.

The Paris Peace Conference of 1919 began a process of dividing the post-war world, and by June that year a Mandate system was put in place by a Covenant of the League of Nations. Article 22 of the Covenant stated that Mandates would be held by 'advanced nations' to govern over peoples not yet ready to 'stand by themselves [in]...the modern world' (Regan, 2017: p73). The Mandate system allowed the division of the Middle East in terms that broadly followed the Sykes-Picot Agreement. Palestine came under British Mandate.

In the inter-war years, with British support, there was a steady (though small) flow of European Jewish settlers who migrated to Palestine to fulfil their national aspirations. In the process, of course, they came into conflict with the national aspirations of the people whose land they were trying to purchase and claim as their own.

As Palestinians fought for their national independence from British imperial rule, Zionist organisations worked side-by-side with the British to suppress Arab political aspirations. During the great Arab Revolt of April 1936 to May 1939, the British deployed 25,000 troops and squadrons of aircraft to crush the rebellion. This was the largest colonial war within the British Empire in the inter-war period. Britain's counter-insurgency campaign was aided and abetted by the European Jewish settlers (Swedenborg, 2003). By the outbreak of the Second World War, British imperialism had 'broken the back' of Palestinian political society, clearing the way for the post-war triumph of Zionism. As Perry Anderson notes, Zionism was:

> A movement of European ethnic nationalism [which] became, inseparably, a form of European overseas colonialism... The Jewish enclave in Palestine was distinctive in another respect too. From the start it was a settler society without a home country—a colony that never issued from a metropolis. Rather, it had a proxy imperialism behind it. British colonial power was the absolute condition of Jewish colonization... Zionism depended completely on the violence of the British imperial state for its growth. (Anderson, 2001)

In response to the imperial carve up of the region, Arab nationalism grew, and culture played a key role. According to Hourani, there was a commitment to the development of:

> a new Arab nation, a new Arab individual...[and] the [artist] should be the 'creator of a new world'. (Hourani, 1991: p396)

For the Syrian writer Ali Ahmad Said (who wrote under the pen-name Adonis), it meant that poetry should aim for "a change in the order of things" (in Jayyusi, 1987: p432). This was a call to update and adapt traditional Arabic poetic forms.

> The basic unit of poetic language should not be the line composed of a fixed number of feet, but the single foot; the accepted system of rhythms—and rhyme itself—could be abandoned; strict syntactical relations between words could give way to looser groupings. Words and images which had been emptied of meaning by repetition should be changed for others and a new system of symbols created. (Hourani, 1991: p396)

This was a call to make poetry and literature less stultified and more accessible and to move away from formal Arabic and adopt local vernacular and idioms: to relate to the experiences of ordinary Arabs by using common symbols and employing recognizable metaphors.

Under Western influence there were also developments in Arab fiction writing. Short stories and novels, which in nineteenth century Arabic writing were often seen as 'entertainment' (meaning, light-weight, fun or frivolous), gradually came to be seen as potentially weighty, with a status and importance almost equivalent to that of poetry. Novels started to engage with the impact of imperial conquest and explored 'national' traditions.

Jabra Ibrahim Jabra's novel *Screaming in a Long Night* (1946) is set towards the end of the British Mandate. In part, it looks at the degradation of city life in contrast to the health and vibrancy of the village. In the background are the British forces and at one point we are told: "On the way a policeman stopped me, a rifle in his hand. He demanded to see my identity card". The city burns. It is presented as a threatening place with few redeeming features. The despondency of the novel is perhaps a reflection of the growing concern, or acknowledgement, that Palestinian society was facing a major crisis point with no clear strategy to resist the Zionist forces or proposed political settlement.

Across the Arab world, the new cultural movement grew to give expression to developing national consciousness. But this was pulled in two directions.

On the one hand there were those who wrote about the dream of a united Arab kingdom. An older verse by Ibrahim al-Yaziji captures some of these feelings:

Awaken O Arabs
For the water has risen up to your stirrups!
What's the use of false hopes
After being so ashamed?
How much more will you be wronged without complaining;
How much more angered without showing anger?
(Quoted in Peled, 1982: p145)

Pan-Arabism would remain a significant political aspiration across the region for much of the twentieth century. It was reflected in the politics of Arab leaders like Gamal Abdul Nasser (1918-1970), political organisations like the Ba'th Party, the Arab League (formed in 1945) and within Palestinian political networks like the Popular Front for the Liberation of Palestine.

On the other hand, after the First World War the division of the Middle East under British and French 'Mandate' led to the formation of independent Arab states, each claiming recognition as separate national entities. This led to *nahda*—or cultural 'awakening'—in many Arab countries, particularly Egypt, Lebanon and Syria.

The cultural movement in the inter-war years was not primarily based in Palestine. Whereas Palestine (and Jerusalem/ Al Quds in particular) had always been significant spiritually for Muslims, Christians and Jews, it was not known as a great artistic and literary centre of the Arab world. Historically, the important Arab administrative, political, cultural and artistic centres were Baghdad, Beirut, Damascus and Cairo. It was here that the new literature started to develop (Masalha, 2018).

Nevertheless, there was an initial flourishing of more patriotic or political writing in Palestine in the inter-war years. During this period:

Literary production inside Palestine was considerable,
and included novels, short stories, plays, both lyrical and
nationalistic, essays, memoirs etc. (Peled, 1982: p150)

In newspapers, magazines and journals, articles started to appear attacking the Mandate authorities, the consequences of growing Jewish migration and land sales to European (Jewish) migrants.

There were two significant Palestinian poets to emerge in these years. The first was Abdulrahim Mahmoud, born in Anabta near Tulkarm, in what is known today as 'the northern sector' of the West Bank. Mahmoud was a teacher and a poet. In 1935 he wrote a poem to welcome Emir Sa'ud ibn Abd al-Aziz (the king of Saudi Arabia) as he passed Anabta. The poem, 'Najm Assoud', pointedly asks:

Have you come to visit the Aqsa Mosque,
Or to bid it farewell before it is lost?

Al Aqsa mosque is in Jerusalem/al-Quds. It is the third holiest site in Islam. But many Jewish people believe it is built on top of the site of the first Temple. As a consequence, the mosque and its grounds continue to be the site of significant conflict between Palestinians and the Israeli state.

'Najm Assoud' reflects the growing concerns in Palestine at that time regarding the impact of European Jewish settlement in the country.

In the great revolt of 1936-39, Abdulrahim Mahmoud joined the ranks of the freedom fighters. Pursued by the British, he fled to Iraq and returned to teaching, this time in Basra. By 1942 he was back in Nablus (a few miles from his Anabta home). Most of his poems were published between then and 1948 in the newspaper *al-Ittihad* and the magazine *al-Ghadd*. Perhaps his most quoted verse comes from the poem 'A Shaheed' (The Martyr).

I shall carry my soul on the palm of my hand
And toss it into the pits of death:
Either a life that pleases a friend
Or a death that enrages the enemy.

The verse points to the need to move beyond words to action in the face of an enemy onslaught. Moving from 'words to deeds' during the Nakba, Mahmoud joined one of the Arab brigades (as part of the volunteer Salvation Army) and fought to defend Palestinian communities in the Galilee. In July,1948 his brigade came under attack from Zionist forces in a battle near Tiberias and Mahmoud was killed. After his death he became known as the 'Martyr poet'.

The second poet of note from this period is Ibrahim Tuqan, older brother of Fadwa. According to Jayyusi (1987), he was the only poet of the time who contributed to the development of new aesthetic values of Palestinian poetry. Salam Mir notes that he blends: "The humorous with the sarcastic, the patriotic with the personal" all of which "affords his poetry a popularity and versatility unmatched by other poets" (Mir, 2013: p17).

Tuqan's poem 'My Homeland' was put to music and became an unofficial Palestinian anthem (and was taken up again by Iraqis after the US-led invasion of 2003). It includes the lines:

My Homeland, My Homeland
Majesty and beauty, sublimity and splendour,
Are in your hills, are in your hills,
…

Our youth will not tire, until your independence
Or they will die, or they will die
We will drink from the cup of death and never be to our enemies
Like slaves, like slaves
…

My homeland, My homeland
The sword and the pen, not talk nor quarrel
Are our symbols, are our symbols
Our glory, Our glory
Is an honourable cause and a waving banner
O, behold you in your eminence
Victorious over your enemies
My homeland, My homeland.
(Alshaer, 2019: pp1/2)

Tuqan's poems may be 'patriotic', urging resistance against both Zionist settlers and British imperialism, but they often include criticism of the Arab elites who collude with imperial interests. In 'My Country', he rages against "My country's brokers", who, he asserts, are a "band who shamefully survive and lead an easy, splendid life". They live in luxury, yet want to portray themselves as Palestine's "saviours" and "protectors".

But they are its ruin
It is bought and sold through their hands
Even the newspapers
Shield them, though we know the truth.
(Jayyusi, 1987: pp318/319)

The first stirrings of 'engaged literature', then, appeared in the inter-war years. This trend was to develop significantly in the post-1948 era.

Edward Said argues that 1948 had a dramatic impact on writing across the Arab world. "No Arab" he argued:

> could say that in 1948 he was in any serious way detached or apart from the events in Palestine. He might reasonably say that he was shielded from Palestine; but he could not say... that he was any less a loser...as a result of what happened in Palestine. (Said, 2000: p46)

The Nakba has been extensively documented by historians such as Pappe (2006), Morris (2008) and Gilmour (1980). Nevertheless, it forms a central part of the story of each of our artists and is the key event in Palestinian history.

At the end of the Second World War, Britain retained its Mandate over Palestine and the end of the war saw increasing numbers of Jewish Holocaust survivors arriving in the country. From 1944, in their pursuit of an independent Jewish state, several groups engaged in a series of attacks on British sites and military personnel. Faced with growing rebellion, the British announced they would end the Mandate no later than August 1948.

As British rule ended, the United Nations proposed the partition of Palestine but the partition resolution was opposed by all the Arab states. The proposal gave 55 percent of Palestine to the creation of a Jewish state and only 45 percent of the land to the majority Palestinian population.

By 1948 the Zionists within Palestine had created, under the British mandate, the key agencies of the state, whose fighting forces were from the start far superior in quality, training and equipment than the combined forces of the Arab armies who were opposed to the proposed partition of Palestine.

On 14 May, 1948, Israel declared its independence and on 15 May the combined armies of Egypt, Syria, Arab League, Transjordan, Iraq and Lebanon attacked. But the outcome of the war was never in serious doubt.

For Israel it was both a war for survival and a means for territorial enlargement beyond the proposed UN borders of 1947. It was successful in achieving both aims, and at the conclusion of the final armistice with Syria in July 1949, Israel had expanded its territory from 55 percent to 79 percent of mandated Palestine (Morris, 2008).

The consequences of both the War and Israel's territorial expansion was devastating for the Palestinian Arabs, who not only had to endure invasion and occupation but were faced with victors who wanted them off 'their' land. It was, as Pappe (2006) has argued, a direct Israeli war whose aim was to permanently remove the indigenous Arab population from the new Israeli state.

A pivotal moment was when the Palestinian village of Deir Yassin was destroyed.

On 9 April, 1948, Jewish forces led by future Israeli prime minister Menachem Begin occupied the village. They sprayed houses with machine guns and the villagers who survived the initial slaughter were herded up and murdered. Many of the women were first raped.

The figures for the numbers killed vary. Palestinian sources suggest it was more than 300; Israeli historians have put the figure at about 170, although recent Israeli estimates put the figure at 93. But as Pappe points out, the Israelis draw a distinction between those killed in the massacre and those killed in the fighting. He observes: "as the Jewish forces regarded any Palestinian village as an enemy military base, the distinction between massacring people and killing them 'in battle' was slight" (Pappe, 2006: p91).

Those that survived "were publicly paraded through Jerusalem in order to spread terror among other sections of the population" (Gilmour, 1980: p69). Deir Yassin was a harbinger of things to come and the brutality of the village's destruction instilled fear in the entire Palestinian community. Jacques de Reynier of the International Red Cross argued that Deir Yassin was hugely significant.

The press and radio spread the news everywhere among Arabs as well as Jews. In this way a general terror was built up among the Arabs, a terror astutely fostered by the Jews. (Quoted in Gilmour, 1980: p100)

In his 1952 Memoirs, Begin says that without Deir Yassin, there would not have been an Israel and that after it, the Zionist forces could "advance like a hot knife through butter" (quoted in Karpf, 2002). And so it proved. As Israeli historian Benny Morris notes:

The principle cause of the mass flight of April-June [1948] was Jewish military attack, or fear of such attack. Almost every instance—exodus from Haifa on April 21-May1; from Jaffa during April-early May; from Tiberius on April 17-18; from Safad on May 10—was the direct and immediate result of an attack on and conquest of Arab neighbourhoods and towns. In no case did a population abandon its homes before an attack; in almost all cases it did so on the very day of an attack and in the days immediately following. And flight proved to be contagious. The fall of, and flight from, the big cities— principally Haifa and Jaffa—radiated pessimism and despair to surrounding villages... Haganah documents described "a psychosis of flight" griping the Palestinian population... The echo of the slaughter on April 9 of the village of Deirdre Yassin...[and] fear that the same fate might befall them propelled villagers to flight. (Morris, 1999: p 255)

The Nakba was destructive of Palestinian life and Palestinian cultural development, and Palestinians were faced with "overcoming the deep sense of alienation resulting from dislocation, dispersion, and oppression" (Elmessari, 1981: p78).

For the hundreds of thousands forced to abandon their homes and flee, theirs was a struggle for daily survival. They were faced with picking up whatever jobs they could, living in slums and refugee camps and struggling to access food and feed their children. Understandably, writing poems and novels was not a priority, but in time the population began to re-engage with the political, social and cultural dynamics of the region.

Those who remained inside Palestine48 found themselves living under military law and were "forcibly cut off from the rest of the Arab world...left without intellectual leadership...separated from the rest of Arab culture" (Elmessari, 1981: pp 77/78).

Gradually, however, Palestinian 'resistance literature' started to develop. Kanafani, Darwish, Tulqan and al-Ali all saw themselves as 'committed artists' and each broadly engaged in what was, in the Arab world, called '*adab al-iltizam*' (literature of commitment).

Adab al-iltizam has its roots in the developing national liberation struggles of the post-World War One era. It demanded an assertion of national identity and history that challenged the dominant imperial narratives of the day. Against the background of the Palestinian Nakba of 1948, Verena Klemm (2000) argues the term adab al-iltizam started to be used in socialist and Palestinian artistic circles. It was argued that literature and art, rather than being something self-referential or merely «art for art's sake», should engage with the masses.

The Egyptian journal al-*Katib al-Misri* initiated a discussion of Sartre's essay Qu'est-ce que la littérature? (What is Literature?). In this essay Sartre argues that there is an inter-play between the writer's freedom and that of the reader.

> Whether he is an essayist, a pamphleteer, a satirist, or a novelist, whether he speaks only of individual passions or whether he attacks the social order...the writer, a free man [sic] addressing free men[sic], has only one subject—freedom... Writing is a certain way of wanting freedom: once you have begun, you are engaged. (Satre, 1947/1978: pp58/59)

For Sartre, then, writing is a commitment or an engagement which should aim to bring about change in the reader and the world. And the suggestion is that 'good' writing has, by its nature, an element of rebellion within it. The writer presents facts, figures, data, knowledge, histories and stories in ways that express truth and challenge the present. As a result, the reader cannot plead ignorance and should be compelled to act. In this way writing involves social responsibility; it is a moral activity.

A further influence on adab al-iltizam came from 'socialist realism'. Socialist realism was a crude, propagandistic form of art promoted in the Soviet Union from the early 1930s. Its aim was to depict heroic workers, peasants, partisans and fighters (nearly always muscular, youthful and determined), to celebrate the glories of socialism and to take an optimistic view on progress towards communism.

Gradually the influence of socialist realism and of Sartre's notion of littérature engagée promoted the assertion that writers should be 'politically committed'.

These themes were refracted in the post-1948 Middle East so that adab al-iltizam came to embody the notion that literature and art had a moral and social role in revealing the nature of society. For Jabra it meant that creative writing had to deal with "freedom, anxiety, protest, struggle, social progress, individual salvation, rebellion, heroism" (Jabra, 1980: p18). This, according to Mattawa (2014), had two specific consequences. First, literature should be written in an accessible way. This involved:

Shorter lines, opposition to classical diction, and the use of everyday images and common objects as symbols. (Mattawa, 2014: pp25/26)

Second, it demanded that writers "engage with the masses and...share in the sufferings and joys of the common people... to portray real life precisely, to explore the struggle between the classes, and to advocate heroism among the oppressed" (Mattawa, 2014: p23).

These themes can be seen at work in Darwish's poem 'Concerning Poetry' (in the collection *Olive Trees*), where he writes:

Comrade poets!
We're in a new world
What's past is dead, who writes a poem

In the age of wind and the atom
Creates prophets!
Our verses
Have no colour
No taste
No sound
If they do not carry the lantern
From house to house!
And if the 'simple' cannot understand our poems
Better for us to shed them
And resort to silence
...
A poet says
If my poems please my friends
And anger my enemies
Then I'm a poet.
And I shall speak!

Palestinian cultural production has been intimately bound up with the process of holding onto ideas of national identity and the struggle for survival. Palestinian resistance and Palestinian cultural production have a long, intertwined history, and, particularly after the establishment of the Palestine Liberation Organisation in 1964, much Palestinian art became a platform for the national liberation movement.

But the 'demand' that writers record and immortalise Palestine and refuse not to be broken or bowed by the occupation can be both a strength and a weakness. As Ashrawi notes, "It can be a compelling force, the dominant spirit of the people and the poetry" or it can degenerate into "mere rhetoric and jargon" (Ashrawai, 1978: p90).

Simple eloquent images taken from everyday life can project a sense of loss and pathos. Samih al-Qassem in his poem "I Speak to the World" (from the collection *The Smoke of Volcanoes*) captures aspects of this when he writes about the sudden eviction of people from place:

I speak about a goat not milked
A morning coffee...not drunk
A mother's dough not baked
A mud roof that flowered

These simple images manage to convey the trauma of eviction and refugeehood. The power of these symbols and this movement in Palestinian cultural production was that it was linked to a growing revolutionary nationalist movement struggling for liberation.

At its best, in the poetry of Darwish for example, adab al-iltizam captures the emotions of the struggle in deeply personal human acts. It takes the emotional, the loving, the sexual, the romantic and connects these feelings to the love of country and to a homeland that has been taken from you or is denied to you in some measure. For a 'homeland' is not primarily a geographical entity, rather it embraces the people we know and love, our relationships to friends and communities and, through these, a connection to a place that has been lost.

This movement in the arts reached its high point in the 1960s and the 1970s when there was, according to Barbara Harlow (1987), a particular alignment of literary positions and organized armed resistance, a marriage of politics and poetics. This does not mean that art was reduced to politics or that it became overly didactic. Rather, in this period, Palestinian cultural production offered a "subtle and esthetically sophisticated portrayal of a genuine existential situation" (Jayyusi, 1992: p72) that aligned with the revolutionary movement for liberation of this period.

But equally we must be aware that the demand for 'commitment' can produce stale and hollow works. In particular, after the dreadful defeat of the PLO forces in Lebanon in 1982, Palestinian political leaders moved from a position of national revolutionary war to one that supported a negotiated peace under the direction of the US. As Hassan (2003) notes:

The years 1982 to 1993 can now be understood as the period when the PLO abandoned politics of resistance linked to those other struggles for national liberation and embraced the politics of appeasement, defined almost entirely in terms of US recognition. (Hassan, 2003: 8)

After the Oslo Accords of 1993, the new Palestinian Authority became the sponsor of 'resistance culture' whilst at the same time trying to 'normalise' relations with Israel and American imperialism. Increasingly, as 'nationalist writing' became the state sponsored writing of the Palestinian Authority, it became detached from the broader revolutionary nationalist movement for change and formulaic and stale.

As time went on, and especially from the early 1990s, some Palestinian poetry became 'stuck' and symbols like 'eagles', 'olive trees', 'the sun', 'the horse' and 'mothers' became frozen symbols of Palestine, freedom, resistance and rebellion, whilst 'the wolf', 'the jailer' and 'chains' became shorthand for the oppressor.

This displays the ways in which cultural production that merely reflects the concerns of adab al-iltizam can quickly become shallow: a crude caricature of the complexities of individuals, of life, of emotions and of the world in which we conduct ourselves.

Kanafani, Darwish, Tuqan and al-Ali produced the majority of their works in the 'classical' nationalist period. Their work fed-off and was part of the movements for liberation. The concerns of adab al-iltizam were not a limit upon their work but, rather, offered an orientation to cultural production within which a rich, diverse and sophisticated set of ideas and writings could develop to produce great art that reveals much about the Palestinian experience.

Chapter 2

The commando who never fired a gun: Ghassan Kanafani

In so far as I am concerned, politics and the novel are an indivisible case and I can categorically state that I became politically committed because I am a novelist, not the opposite.

Our style of operation is not an invention of a person but the result of our situation. If we could liberate Palestine by standing on the borders of South Lebanon and throwing roses on the Israelis, we would do it. It is nicer. But I don't think it will work.

(Kanafani, Quoted in Rosen, 1974: p3)

GHASSAN KANAFANI WAS BORN in the port city of Akka (Acre) on 9 April, 1936. Acre is in Haifa Bay in the Galilee, on the Northern Mediterranean coast of Palestine48. It is roughly half-way between the city of Haifa and the Lebanese border. In the UN Partition Plan (adopted as General Assembly Resolution 181, 9 November, 1947) Acre would have remained within an Arab (Palestinian) state.

In the 1930s, Acre was an expanding city. Under the British Mandate its population had grown from 6,420, according to the 1922 census (4,883 of whom were Muslim; 1,344 Christian; 102 Baha'i; 78 Jewish and thirteen Druze), to close to 18,000 (overwhelmingly Muslim) when the British left in May 1948 (Hadawi, 1970: p40).

Kanafani's birth coincided with the start of what is known as *al-thawra al-kubra* (the Great Revolt) of 1936-39. This was the most important anti-colonial struggle against British rule in the Middle East in the inter-war era (Swedenborg, 2003).

On 13 April, 1936, against a background of escalating Jewish-Arab skirmishes and the imposition of a state of emergency by the British colonial power, Palestinians launched a General Strike that would last six months. The strike was coordinated through National Committees that sprung up in villages, towns and cities across the country. On 25 April, a Higher Arab Committee was established and presented their demands to the British. These demands were (1) end European Jewish migration to Palestine, (2) stop land sales (ie of Palestinian land) to Jewish organisations and settlers and (3) grant Palestine its independence.

42 The Revolt quickly spread and became an armed uprising that would last until 1939. By mid-1938, the insurgents had control of the highlands and most Palestinian urban centres. The British responded with their customary brutality, deploying 20,000 troops. The RAF were unleashed on Arab centres and Zionist auxiliaries were recruited and armed to enforce colonial law and order. This armed European settler community were acting in both their and their imperial master's interests.

Acre prison housed hundreds of Palestinian prisoners during the revolt. Over 100 Arabs were executed by the British, many for merely being in possession of a gun or even a weapon cartridge.

Kanafani's father and several relatives were actively involved in the revolt as it spread across the country (Brehony, 2017). Thus, Kanafani's early years were immersed in the developing Palestinian struggle for freedom. Later, he would write a history of the Revolt that would be shaped by his distinctive political approach. 'Between 1936 and 1939', he wrote:

the Palestinian revolutionary movement suffered a severe setback at the hands of three separate enemies that were to constitute together the principle threat to the nationalist movement in Palestine in all subsequent stages of its struggle: the local reactionary leadership; the regimes in the Arab states surrounding Palestine; and the imperialist-Zionist enemy. (Kanafani, 1972)

Kanafani would incorporate these themes in much of his later creative writing: the problem of weak Palestinian leadership, the role of corrupt Arab states turning their back on Palestinians and their own people, and the impact of imperial intervention and Zionist colonial settlement on the region.

The Revolt also produced one of Palestine's most popular 'resistance' lyrics which was memorised by Palestinians and passed on by word of mouth. It was originally extemporised by an anonymous Palestinian just before his execution by the British, and was reproduced by Kanafani in his review *Resistance Literature in Occupied Palestine* (1948-66):

Night: let the captive finish his song.
By dawn his wing will flutter
And the hanged one will swing
With the wind.

Night: slow your pace.
Let me pour out my heart to you,
Perhaps you have forgotten who I am
And what my troubles are.

Pity, how my hours have slipped
Down your hands

Do not think I weep from fear.
My tears are for my country
And for my fledgling children,
Hungry at home
Without their father.

Who will feed them after me?
My two brothers
Before me swung on the scaffold.

And how will my wife spend her days,
Lonely and in tears?
I did not even leave a bracelet

Round her wrist
When my country cried for arms.

(Anonymous, 1936)

Ghassan Kanafani

This poem is used by Kanafani to emphasise how, under repressive conditions of occupation, popular poetry that uses accessible language and "is easier to learn by heart, and quicker to appeal to the sentiments" forms a key element of resistance literature. It easily "spreads from mouth to mouth and lives without publication" (Kanafani in Hijjawi, 1968: pp4,5). This approach is one that would help shape his later writings.

Ghassan was the third child to be born into the Kanafani family and would eventually be joined by a further three siblings. The family were comfortably well-off. His father was a lawyer and, like many Palestinian children from his background, Ghassan was sent to a French missionary school where he was taught in French rather than Arabic.

But like all Palestinians, Ghassan's life changed directly because of the ethnic cleansing of 1947/48.

On his twelfth birthday (9 April, 1948), Zionist forces attacked the Palestinian village of Deir Yassin (see chapter 1 above). The date of Deir Yassin's destruction was etched on the minds of all Palestinians. According to Anni Kanafani (1973), Ghassan's widow, after the events when he was twelve, Ghassan never again celebrated a birthday.

The following month the Nakba came to Acre. The city had shown great resilience in the face of shelling from Zionist forces, but then the Hagana (a paramilitary organisation set up in Mandate Palestine) resorted to biological warfare.

The city's main water supply, an aqueduct from the Kabri springs, was injected with typhoid germs. The International Red Cross were guarded about apportioning blame for the sudden outbreak of the deadly disease and stated it was the result of "outside poisoning". The British forces in the city concluded the infection was undoubtedly waterborne and not due to over-crowding or unhygienic conditions, as the Hagana claimed. Indeed 55 British soldiers had to be transferred from the city after they were struck with the disease (Pappe, 2006, p100).

The Carmeli Brigade, notorious for their butchery in Haifa, then prepared to attack the city. They attacked with shells and started to blast the city with loudspeakers telling the inhabitants to "surrender or commit suicide" otherwise "we will destroy you to the last man" (Morris, 2008: p166).

In the face of intensive shelling, typhoid and the loudspeaker threats, people began to flee.

Twelve-year-old Ghassan took to the road with his family. He was now a refugee. The family travelled first to a village in southern Lebanon, then on to Beirut, onwards to the mountains outside Damascus, before finally settling in the Damascus ghetto.

Like most Palestinian refugees, the Kanafanis thought they would soon return home, but this was to be a permanent exile: their former comfortable life was replaced with one of poverty and hardship.

The teenage Ghassan began to paint, draw and write notes about his life and what he saw about him amongst Palestinian refugees (Riley, 2000).

In Damascus he returned to schooling. After completing his initial studies, he worked as a teacher at an UNRWA school. UNRWA is the United Nations Relief and Works Agency for Palestine Refugees in the Near East and was formed in 1949. Whilst teaching refugee children, two events had a significant impact upon him.

First, he noticed that his students were often falling asleep during class. When he investigated, he found that many of the children were working late into the evening to try and help supplement their family's meagre earnings. As he noted:

I realised that the children's drowsiness did not stem from scorn for me or dislike of their studies, nor did it have anything to do with my capacity as a teacher. It was simply the reflection of a political problem. (in Riley, 2000: p3)

The second incident occurred when he was teaching the children to draw an apple and banana, part of the set curriculum. He suddenly realised that the children had never seen either of those fruits, an astonishing revelation for someone from

Palestine, rich with all manner of fruit and vegetables. He then turned to asking them to draw things that they saw in the refugee camp.

He would later describe these events as a "decisive turning point" in his life; a recognition of the impact of exile on refugees and an understanding of what the sociologist C. Wright Mills called the socio-political 'public causes' of private pain and trauma that so many of the refugees felt and experienced (Wright Mills, 1959).

Whilst teaching, Kanafani enrolled at Damascus University to study Arabic literature. At University, he began to write short stories about the plight of Palestinians. He joined a literary society called the League of Literature and Life (Riley, 2003). Amongst his university colleagues within the League, he was noted for his determination to get his stories published. His stories spoke of the immediate, of the plight of Palestinians and of Arabs more generally. He was determined they should be published in magazines or journals because they spoke to the Palestinian crisis, because, as he said, for him "politics and the novel are an indivisible case" (Rosen, 1974: p3).

University also brought him to more directly active political engagement.

Whilst a student, Kanafani met George Habash (1926-2008), who was at the time the leader of the Arab Nationalist Movement. Habash was to become a significant Palestinian leader and was an important influence on Kanafani. Their political relationship developed during the second half of the 1950s, but Kanafani would work closely with Habash throughout the rest of his life.

Habash was born in Lydda, part of present-day Tel Aviv, to an Orthodox Christian family. When the Nakba took place in 1948, he was at the American University in Beirut. He rushed home to act as a medical orderly as the Zionist forces advanced on his town and cleansed it of its Arab inhabitants. After displacement, he went back to his studies and in 1951 he graduated as a medic.

The Arab Nationalist Movement was formally set up in Amman in 1956. It was a pan-Arabist movement whose slogan was "Unity, Liberation, Revenge". The slogan referred to the 'unity' of Arab people's and countries and 'liberation' from Western imperialism, whilst 'revenge' referred to the recovery of a free Palestine. Habash was:

> Influenced by Baathism, a pan-Arab version of socialism taking root in Syria and Iraq, and by the revolutionary tide beginning to sweep the Third World. (Walker & Gowers, 2003: p 12)

Pan-Arabism was particularly significant in the early Palestinian movement. This was partly because of the scale of the defeat inflicted on the Palestinians by the Nakba and the resultant discrediting of the former Palestinian leadership. Together these two elements meant that many activists were drawn to pan-Arabism as the road to Palestinian liberation; it seemed to offer the prospect of liberation through the combined forces of Arab states and armies, rather than merely relying on the self-activity of Palestinians themselves. As Hourani notes:

> Since 1948 the Palestinians themselves had not been able to play an independent part in the discussions about their own destiny: their leadership had collapsed, they were scattered between a number of states, and those who had lost their homes and work had to make a new life for themselves. They had been able to play a part only under the control of the Arab states and with their permission. (Hourani, 1991: p412)

Pan-Arabism was attractive for several reasons.

First, it emphasised Arab unity. It asserted that the common history, culture and language of the Arab peoples created the possibility of close political union and, as a result, greater collective power on the global stage.

Second, linked to the idea of Arab unity was the notion that a unified Arab block could effectively stand alongside other post-colonial societies to create an alternative political network, part of the Third World, that would not be committed to or under undue pressure from the two great empirical powers east and west, the US and the USSR, in the Cold War era.

Third, in Egypt and in the persona of Gamal Abdel Nasser Hussein, pan-Arabism had a strong political leader. Nasser had overthrown a corrupt King (in 1952), chased out the French, British and Israeli forces from Suez (1956), adopted socialist economic measures (very broadly meaning land reform, nationalisation of the Suez Canal, the building of the Aswan Dam, greater demand management of the economy and, limited, social reforms) and, in 1958, joined with Syria to establish the United Arab Republic (UAR). The UAR then entered a looser federation with Yemen. With the Iraqi revolution of 1958, there was the possibility of Iraq joining the UAR. For a brief period, until its dissolution in 1961, the dream of political unity seemed a very real possibility. And a United Arab Republic, for some, established a strong counterweight to the military power of Israel.

Finally, for some pan-Arabists this in turn was reinforced by the successes of a range of post-war anti colonial struggles that erupted in the post Second World War era. The success of the revolutions in, for example, Ghana (1957), Cuba (1959), Kenya (1960), Algeria (1962) and Yemen (1962) alongside the Vietnamese struggle against first the French then the Americans provided inspiration for those involved in anti-imperialist conflicts. They pointed to the possibility and potential for armed struggles to liberate colonies from their imperial masters.

However, for the majority of those who described themselves as pan-Arabists at this point, Palestinian liberation would come through alliances with strong Arab leaders—not (yet) through commitment to the armed struggle. As Hirst notes:

Habash...saw in Nasser the instrument of Arab unity and the liberation of Palestine through a conventional war he would fight in his own good time. (Hirst, 2003: p407)

Between 1955 and 1960, Kanafani taught in Kuwait, where he began writing novellas and short stories, including 'Letter from Gaza' (1956) and 'The Land of Sad Oranges' (1958).

In his writing, the pan-Arabist Kanafani set out to do three key things. First, to tell the Palestinian story, to ensure the

Palestinian voice is heard and not forgotten. Second, to establish the reality of the place, Palestine, and assert its history and the Palestinian sense of belonging. Third, to give expression to the dislocation of exile and to the contradictory feelings and sense of self this creates.

The Land of Sad Oranges is Palestine. In this short story Kanafani looks at how exile shapes the notion of home, of Palestine itself.

The story tells of the suffering of a middle-class family expelled from their home during the Nakba. First, they move from Jaffa to Acre and then are forced to flee to Lebanon. Told through the eyes of a child, it tells of the families rushed, chaotic escape from Acre. The story starts by recalling the first stage of exile. "When we set out from Jaffa for Acre, there was nothing tragic about our departure... I...enjoyed those days because they kept me from school". But then things changed:

> But...the picture gradually became clearer on the night of the great attack on Acre. That night passed, cruel and bitter, amidst the despondency of the men and the tears of the women. You and I and the others of our age were too young to understand what the story meant from beginning to end, but that night the threads began to grow clearer. In the morning, when the Jews withdrew, threatening and fuming, a big lorry was standing at the door of our house. A simple collection of bedding was being thrown into it, from here and there, feverishly... I saw your mother climb into the lorry, followed by your aunt and the children. Your father started tossing you and your brothers and sisters into the lorry, and on top of the belongings, and then he seized me...and lifted me over his head into the iron rack on the roof of the driver's cab, where I found my brother Riyad sitting quietly. The lorry was already moving off before I had settled myself... Beloved Acre was already disappearing behind the bends in the road going up to *Ras Naquora* (Kanafani, 1999: p75)

Ras Naquora was the checkpoint at the Lebanese border.

There the family encounter an orange seller and it is this event that brings home the reality of their loss. They stare at the oranges, remembering the trees and groves that they tended for so long but which are now abandoned to the Israelis. The story progresses and tells of the family's impoverishment, isolation and desperation. The father has a breakdown and considers suicide, and even considers killing his children before he takes his life. As he lies in his bed, revolver at his side, there is an orange "dried up and shrivelled" (Kanafani, 1999: p80).

In a few pages, Kanafani manages to dramatically emphasise how exile shapes the notion of the absent place, Palestine, and captures the immense suffering of the refugees. He does so in a way that tells the tale without embellishment. Reflecting the themes of adab al-iltizam, the style is one he would maintain in most of his writing: short, clipped sentences, an economy of expression, but with, as Khoury notes, "the immediacy of theatrical space" (Khoury, 2013: p89).

'Letter from Gaza' addresses a theme which remains pertinent for many Palestinians today: whether it is better for oneself and immediate family to leave Palestine and make a life somewhere else in the world or whether one should stay and fight in the hope of fulfilling the dream of a liberated Palestine.

The letter is written by an unknown author to his close friend Mustafa. Mustafa has left Palestine and gone to the US, via Kuwait. The US, Mustafa claims, is a place where, "there is greenery, water and lovely faces" (Kanafani, 1999: p111) and now he hopes his friend will join him, fulfilling their early life-plans to work hard and leave Palestine, to enrich themselves and have a freer life 'outside'.

The letter begins with the author acknowledging their shared dream to move to the USA and Mustafa's invitation for him to stay with him in Sacramento. Further, he imparts the exciting news that he has been offered a job in the Department of Civil Engineering at the University of California.

But quickly the author lets his friend know his mind is made up: he will not be joining him.

Throughout, the letter flits back and forth between the present and the correspondents' shared past. It takes the reader through the hardship of refugee life, the suffocating oppression of life as one of the dispossessed and the impact of forced migration moving across the Middle East to earn a living. He recalls their time in Kuwait working in a school, Mustafa working for the Kuwaiti Ministry for Education, the author struggling on the meagre wages at an UNWRA school. "My life", he says in a passage that captures alienated existence wonderfully:

> had a gluey, vacuous quality as though I were a small oyster, lost in oppressive loneliness, slowly struggling with a future as dark as the beginning of the night, caught in a rotten routine, a spewed-out combat with time... There was a slipperiness to my whole life, it was all a hankering for the end of the month. (Kanafani, 1999: p112)

There was an attraction, he notes, of the possibility of "liberat[ing] myself...in green California, far from the reek of defeat that for seven years has filled my nostrils" (Kanafani, 1999: p113). So, he returned to Gaza for a holiday before he left for the US. Gaza was "more cramped than the mind of a sleeper in the throes of a fearful nightmare, with its narrow streets that had their peculiar smell, the smell of defeat and poverty" (Kanafani, 1999: p113).

The early passages of the letter succinctly capture the stultifying oppression of refugee life and the dream of freedom elsewhere.

But then his sister-in-law asks him to accompany her to the hospital to visit his niece, "Nadia...my brother's beautiful thirteen-year-old daughter" (Kanafani, 1999:p113).

His visit to the hospital is traumatic.

He sees the child lying on a hospital bed and when she realises it's her uncle, she asks if he has brought her any presents. He lies: "Nadia, I've brought you presents from Kuwait, lots of presents. I will wait till you can leave your bed, completely well and healed... I've bought you the red trousers you wrote and asked me for" (Kanafani, 1999: p114).

Ghassan Kanafani

There is an excruciating silence. Nadia says nothing but pulls back the bedcovers and points to the space where her leg used to be.

The rest of the letter tells Nadia's story. She lost her leg because she threw herself on top of her younger brothers and sisters to protect them from the Israeli bombs. She could have run away and saved herself but she didn't. "Why?" he asks.

So, no, the author tells us, he will not leave to save himself but will stay "among the ugly debris of defeat". And to Mustafa he urges:

Return to us! Come back, to learn from Nadia's leg,
amputated from the top of the thigh, what life is and what
existence is worth. Come back, my friend. We are all waiting
for you. (Kanafani, 1999: p115)

In May 2008, as part of the Palestine Festival of Literature, John Berger read Kanafani's 'Letter from Gaza'. Berger's powerful, emotional reading, available online, took place at the mid-point between the Israeli assaults on Gaza in 2006 and 2009. Berger is almost in tears as he reads the final, compelling paragraph, "learn from Nadia's leg...what life is and what existence is worth".

Today it is difficult to read Kanafani's Letter and not be reminded of the deaths and maiming of children that have been inflicted by the IDF. Defence of Children International (Palestine) noted that in 2018 the IDF killed an average of just over one child every week and that 183 children had been injured by Israeli forces, with 130 of these taking place in Gaza. Nineteen of these children suffered permanent disability because of their injuries (DCIP, 2018). Nadia speaks to generations of Palestinians who have been disabled by Israeli forces and "Letter from Gaza" remains as powerful today as it was when it was written in 1956.

In 1960 George Habash persuaded Kanafani to move again, this time to Beirut to become a journalist and start working on the pro-Nasserist daily paper *al-Muharrir* (The Liberator). This publication included a weekly supplement which he also edited called Filastin (Palestine). He was also invited to join the editorial board of Habash's political journal *al-Hurriyya* (Independence).

It was whilst working as a journalist in Beirut in this period that Kanafani published his most famous novella *Men in the Sun* (1962) and, perhaps his most interesting novel stylistically, *All That is Left to You* (1966).

Men in the Sun covers a few days in the life of four travelling companions who are trying to get from Iraq to Kuwait. The plot is straightforward. Three of the men have left Jordan: Abu Qais is an old man, Assad a young man and Marwan a youth. Each is escaping across the desert in search of work and a better life in Kuwait and each leave behind a story of sorrow, despair and suffering as a consequence of the Nakba.

The novella moves back and forth across time to tell each man's story and what brought him to this point of 'escape'. The move to Kuwait seems to offer salvation from their present situation; they cannot exist in their past because they have been expelled from their land during the Nakba; they have no present because they are 'non-entities', refugees without papers or legal status; escape to Kuwait seems to offer a road to redemption. Each individual story flows into the broader narrative as it unfolds.

The possibility of 'escape', of leaving Palestine and trying to make a better life elsewhere, was debated in 'Letter from Gaza'. It also features in some of Kanafani's other short stories, such as 'Death of Bed 12' (1961), where Muhammad Ali Akbar undertakes a journey to make a new life:

> ...he had the promise of a new life in Kuwait. In a year or two he'd return to Oman and swagger through the alleys of Ibkha wearing a brilliant white aba with a golden hem, like the one he'd seen draped across the shoulders of one of the notables...
> (Kanafani, 1999: p120)

But rather than fame and fortune, Muhammad Ali Akbar faces hardship and an anonymous death in a Kuwaiti hospital.

Kanafani seems to be suggesting that life away from one's country, especially for those forced into migration, whether for political or, in the case of Muhammad Ali Akbar, economic reasons, rarely leads to fulfilled dreams. And so, the story plays out in *Men in the Sun*.

Each of the three refugees arrives in Basra, where they meet with 'the fat man'. The fat man is a people smuggler, preying on the vulnerable, whose charges for getting the men across the border are beyond each man's reach.

But all is not lost. A Palestinian truck driver, Abu Khaizuran, who also has a back-story of serious injury when he was castrated by a shell in battle during the Nakba, agrees to take the three men to Kuwait hidden in his empty water truck.

The journey starts smoothly. The three men, hidden inside the truck, get across the Iraqi border in seven minutes. But things unravel at the Kuwaiti checkpoint. The border guards take an age to sign Abu Khaizuran's papers, and use the time to humiliate him about a supposed illicit relationship he has in Basra; his humiliation made worse by the fact of his castration. The truck is left in the burning sun.

Eventually allowed on his way, Abu Khaizuran drives as fast as he can. When out of sight the checkpoint, he slams on his breaks but, foretelling the disaster that awaits, the "wheels set up a screech like a howl" (Kanafani, 1999: p70). The three men are dead. Abu Khaizuran dumps their bodies and takes their possessions. The novella ends with Abu Khaizuran asking a question:

> Why didn't you knock on the sides of the tank? Why didn't you bang the sides of the tank? Why? Why? Why? (Kanafani, 1999: p74)

The disaster of *Men in the Sun* represents the larger disaster of the Nakba. The novella is full of dreams and false hopes that are repeatedly crushed by despair. The three men are bought and sold by agents and fellow Palestinians, none of whom have a plan that can succeed. They are killed by the sun but they do not see it, they are literally kept in the dark.

Abu Khaizuran represents the Palestinian leadership,

castrated, ineffectual and leading the men to disaster. Even his name, Khaizuran, is significant. It means 'bamboo', hard on the outside but hollow and without a central core.

The border guards represent the Arab leadership. Despite dealing with a driver whom, we are told, is respected, they disrespect and jeer at Abu Khaizuran, their air-conditioned room a sharp contrast to the stifling, murderous heat building up in the tank. And the men do not bang on the tank because no-one listens to the voice of refugees, the voiceless and oppressed of the region.

Kanafani skillfully uses "multiple time frames" to portray refugees searching "for a tangible identity". In the process he:

> presents his stories rather than telling them from the viewpoint of an omnipresent omniscient narrator. He creates the circumstances, sets the stage and allows the characters to perform their drama without interrupting or making any comment. (Magrath, 1979: p106)

Men in the Sun is a realist tragedy. It is a compelling, accessible story that demands not only recognition of the plight of Palestinian refugees but also a more resolute leadership from Palestinian and, more generally, Arab politicians.

The Palestinian political situation was gradually starting to shift in the mid-1960s. In 1964 the Arab League moved to set up a separate Palestinian entity, which they called the Palestine Liberation Organisation (PLO). The PLO was initially under Egyptian control. For its first four years it was a weak and ineffectual organisation.

New Year's Day, 1965, saw another significant event. Beirut newspapers received a notice, the Al-Asifa Communique Number One. Essentially this was the first announcement of military action by a small Palestinian grouping called Fatah under the leadership of Yasser Arafat.

This led to an increasing debate in Palestinian circles over guerrilla warfare and the armed struggle. A number, including Kanafani, started to look at other Third World, anti-colonial liberation struggles for inspiration. The ideas of Mao started to gain a foothold amongst some activists. Indeed, Kanafani made two visits to China in 1965 and 1966. The attraction of Mao for many Palestinian fidayeen was the apparent commitment to militant struggle for liberation and 'living the revolution' based on ideals of simple egalitarian peasant living and hard work.

Many of these debates were aired in the bi-monthly magazine Filastin, which Kanafani was editing at the time. These debates would eventually result in Kanafani helping to found the PFLP in 1967. But they also played out in his creative writing.

All That's Left to You (1966) was published against the backdrop of these debates. It won Kanafani the Lebanese Literature Prize for 1966. It is an ambitious and technically complex novel in which both 'time' and 'the desert' are considered characters alongside Maryam, her brother Hamid and husband Zakaria.

The events of the novel take place over eighteen hours, though flash backs are used to allow Kanafani to provide details of his characters earlier lives.

Maryam and Hamed live in a Gaza refugee camp. They lost their father fifteen years earlier during the Nakba and, in the chaos of the time, they got separated from their mother, who ended up in Jordan. Between the children and their mother lies the Negev desert, occupied and patrolled by Israeli soldiers.

Before he died, their father asked Maryam, who was 20 at the time, not to marry until the conflict had been resolved. Hamid, ten years younger than Maryam, has been tasked with finding her a husband but his inactivity seems to indicate his passive agreement with his father.

But then Maryam announces she is pregnant and that she intends to marry the child's father, Zakaria. Zakaria already has a wife and five children with a sixth on its way. Whilst they marry, Zakaria tells Maryam she must abort their child and Maryam has to confront the reality of being a second wife. Subsequently Zakaria tells Maryam he will divorce her unless she aborts the child.

The siblings blame each other for their situation. During Maryam and Zakaria's marriage ceremony, Hamid decides to leave Gaza and cross the desert to be with his mother.

It is not only Zakaria's 'ensnaring' of Maryam that pushes Hamid to leave. We also learn that he is a traitor whoidentified Salim, a Palestinian fidayeen (freedom fighter), to Israeli troops to protect himself. The Israelis threaten to kill several Palestinian men from the refugee camp in reprisal for Salim's actions. Zakaria was "prostrate at the officer's feet...awaiting the terrible moment of death" when he shouted:

"I'll show you Salim!" Salim had spared him the full role of traitor by firmly stepping three paces forward and standing there. (Kanafani, 2004: p.38)

As a result, Salim is executed.

We learn that Salim had asked Hamid to join the fidayeen, but Hamid prevaricated. Inaction and prevarication are his way in both personal and political life.

On his journey across the desert, Hamid stumbles across an Israeli soldier. Hamid disarms him, throws away his machine gun and holds him at knife point. This action is not the result of conscious choice and challenging the enemy. Rather, Hamid is forced by circumstances to overthrow the soldier, and the soldier does not struggle much because he assumes this is a joke being played on him by his friends.

As the story comes to its climax. Maryam takes control of her situation and plunges a knife into Zakaria, her personal oppressor as well as a traitor: the enemy within. Hamid, as the sun rises on the desert, plunges the knife into the Israeli soldier, but rather than a conscious act of rebellion and resistance, it is an act of desperation. It is now clear that by throwing away the machine gun but keeping the knife, Hamid sees his actions as an act of personal salvation not part of the collective struggle against the occupier. As Coffin notes:

Violence was, for Kanafani, a necessary and unavoidable part of [the] resistance, but ideally, it should be goal-oriented and undertaken with a clear sense of commitment to the common cause. (Coffin, 1996: p.115)

Kanafani's use of the five main characters in the novel works to pull the story together and provide depth to the eighteen hours of the narrative. He uses the desert as a means of observing and commenting on Hamid's journey, his helplessness and his courage. By focussing on the five characters, Kanafani tells us, he is able to create:

> A series of disconnected lines which occasionally come together in such a way they seem to be making just two strands and no more. This process of fusion also involves the elements of time and place, so that there appears to be no clear distinction between places and times which are far removed from each other, or indeed between places and times at a single moment. (Kanafani, 2004: p. xxi)

Time is symbolised by the ticking of the clock in Maryam and Zakaria's temporary home in the Gaza refugee camp, by Hamid's watch as he crosses the Negev desert and even by the beat of the earth after he has thrown his watch away.

Times and places are often juxtaposed in the narrative to cover separate significant events. In the English language version of the novel, different type faces are used when the different characters narrate events. Thus, in the passage below, the desert speaks first (in italics) about Hamid's chaotic journey across the Negev, followed by Maryam (in bold) discussing an earlier attempt by Zakaria to meet with Hamid to discuss their proposed marriage:

> *He had abandoned any kind of reflection and was relying on senses distorted by terror and excitement. He seemed, from his emotions, like an intrepid adventurer who dares to knock on an unknown gate/* **When I saw him at the door, I felt afraid and excited at the same time, and trembled all over. Hamid had left only five minutes before, and Zakaria, self-assured, was standing in the doorway asking, "is he here?"** (Kanafani, 2004: pp12-13)

The novel's innovative and experimental form took Palestinian writing to a new level and, for this reason, *All That's Left to You* is

58

noted as one of the great post-Nakba Arab novels.

The novel, published in 1966, coincided with increasing military operations by, primarily, Fatah. At the time, these operations were small and contentious. Pan-Arabists like Habash were initially opposed to such 'adventures' and demanded resistance operations be under Egyptian control. But soon three events were to reshape Palestinian liberation politics fundamentally.

First, there was the Six Day War of May 1967. Referred to as the *Naksa*, the swift Israeli military victory dealt a massive blow to those who looked to the Arab regimes, especially Egypt and Syria, to help liberate Palestine. The war was a catastrophic defeat for the Arab states. It allowed the Israelis to expand their borders, taking the West Bank from Jordan, the Golan Heights from Syria and the Sinai peninsula from Egypt. Of course, it also led to a second wave of Palestinian displacement.

These events led many to re-evaluate their approach. George Habash recalled:

I think that the first time we saw that they [Fatah] were right was after 1967. Only after that did we feel that the conditions were right for a Palestinian armed struggle. (Walker & Towers, 2003: p46)

As a result, Habash formed the Popular Front for the Liberation of Palestine (PFLP) in December 1967. In its inaugural statement of 11 December, the PFLP declared:

The only language which the enemy understands is that of revolutionary violence...the historic task is...[to open a fierce struggle against the occupier] thereby turning the occupied territories into an inferno whose fires consume the usurpers. (Hirst, 2003: p410)

Kanafani became one of the key leaders of the organisation. The PFLP adopted Marxism, committed itself to the armed struggle and set itself against any solution except the liberation of Palestine48 'from the river to the sea'.

The PFLP's official political stance was Marxism-Leninism.

What this meant is perhaps best revealed by the Habash's reading when he was imprisoned in Syria for ten months in 1968. Near the top of the list were works by Ho Chi Minh and Mao. The Marxism of Habash and the PFLP was, then, heavily influenced by Third World anticolonial armed struggles. This was not the classical Marxism of Lenin and Trotsky with its emphasis on the self-emancipation of the working class.

Second, although the Six Day War was a disaster for the Arab regimes, it did not stop guerrilla attacks on Israel from Palestinian militants. In fact, the number of cross-border skirmishes, from Jordan and Lebanon, increased. Palestinian fighters were becoming better trained and armed. The Israelis vowed revenge.

In March 1968, Israeli forces (15,000 troops and tanks) amassed on the Jordanian border. Their mission was to destroy the Palestinian base at Karameh in west-central Jordan. The Jordanian government urged a tactical retreat. Arafat, however, drew his fighters together and reportedly told them:

> Our Arab nation has been escaping and fleeing
> continuously... We have to prove to the Israeli enemy that
> there are people who will not flee. We are going to confront
> him in the same way that David confronted Goliath. (quoted
> in Walker & Towers, 2003: p 50).

Fighters from the PFLP moved into the hills, where they took Israeli paratroops by surprise. The Jordanian army pounded the Israeli lines. Three hundred Fatah fighters stood their ground against the Israeli frontal assault. One of the fighters wired himself up as a suicide bomb and hurled himself at an Israeli tank. Seventeen other men dug themselves in and confronted Israeli tanks with rocket-propelled grenades, and all but one died. The seventeen became immortalised in the name of Arafat's future security service, Force 17.

After heavy fighting, the Israelis withdrew; 28 Israelis had been killed, 69 were injured and 33 tanks had been destroyed. Although 90 Palestinians were killed and the Palestinian camp at

Karameh had been destroyed, the battle was a huge ideological victory for the Palestinian fighters and Fatah in particular. As Neff notes:

The battle of Karameh sent a surge of optimism through the Palestinian community and established the Palestinians' claim to being a national liberation organization. Karameh also was a forceful refutation of the claim by some Israelis that Palestinians did not exist. They had at last enlarged the conflict beyond a contest between refugee and Israeli into a revolutionary context where they were widely regarded, particularly in the Third World, as an authentic political movement. (Neff, 1998)

Finally, as Fatah grew, so did the influence of Arafat. In January 1969, the PLO came under the control of the guerrilla organisations, and of Arafat. Arafat wanted the PLO to be a United Front of Palestinian organisations and so it gradually became an umbrella organisation under the control of Fatah, but with the PFLP and other Palestinian groups in its ranks.

In June 1967 shortly after the Six Day War, Kanafani left his job on al-Muharrir to join the daily *al-Anwar* (The Lights) as editor of its weekly magazine.

By 1969 he had moved again. He was now playing a leading role within the PFLP. He was their media spokesperson and he moved to found and edit the PFLP journal *al-Hadaf* (The Goal). His journalistic writing was insightful and offered a first line defence of the armed struggle and of the PFLP.

This included defence of the PFLP tactic of hijacking Israeli and Western airplanes to draw attention to the plight of the Palestinian refugees, which was a controversial tactic that drew criticism from other Palestinian groups as well as from the international solidarity movement. But Kanafani was unrepentant, describing the hijackings as "one of the most correct things we ever did" (Carleton, 1970).

He was responsible for the official PFLP statement that appeared in *Der Stern* on 16 September 1970:

When we hijack a plane, it has more effect than if we kill a hundred Israelis in battle. For decades world public opinion has been neither for nor against the Palestinians. It simply ignored us. At least the world is talking about us now.

Kanafani was also outspoken in his opposition to talks with the Israeli government. Famously, in a 1970 interview broadcast with the Australian broadcaster Richard Carleton, Kanafani described the prospect of peace talks between Israel and Palestinians as a "capitulation" and akin to a conversation between "a sword and a neck" (Carleton, 1970).

The changing context of post-Naksa Palestinian politics also brought about a change in Kanafani's writing. He wrote several short pieces about life in the refugee camps, including *The Child Goes to the Camp* (1967), *A Present for the Holiday* (1968) and *Guns in the Camp* (1969). In 1969 he published two important pieces *Returning to Haifa* and *Umm Saad*.

Umm Saad, means Saad's mother. She appears in a series of stories that mark a change of direction in Kanafani's writing. Reflecting Kanafani's political turn, the stories to some degree reflect the influence of socialist realism. Umm Saad is an epic hero of the Palestinian struggle. For Kanafani, she is a symbol of the growing revolutionary consciousness of the Palestinian refugees, the sons and daughters of the land of Palestine.

According to Kanafani, she was "a real woman, whom I know well, whom I see regularly and to whom I am somehow related", but he goes on:

> Nevertheless, Umm Saad is not an individual woman. If it were not that she, through her body, her mind and her labour, incorporates the heart of the masses, the soul of their concerns, and an indivisible part of their daily lives, she could not possibly be what she is. Thus, for me, the voice has always been the voice of the Palestinian class which has paid dearly the price of defeat, that class which now stands under the sky of wretchedness and misery in the forefront of the battle, and resists, continuing to resist the most of all. (Quote in Coffin, 1996: p112)

Umm Saad, then, is the embodiment of Palestinian refugee women of the camps. Her character is strong, resourceful and steadfast.

> She has lived for a crushing load of years in the torment of the camps... She is a woman of about forty...with a strength greater than a rock and a patience more than endurance itself... she toil[s] to snatch for herself and her children an honest bit to eat... When she knocks on the door...I am enveloped in the smell of the camps, in their misery and deep-routed steadfastness, their poverty and hopes. (Kanafani, 2000: p99)

She is also the mother of a fidayeen:

> I told the woman sitting beside me on the bus that my son had become a combatant. I told her that I loved him and missed him, but he was a true son of his mother. (Kanafani, 2000: p101)

Indeed, in *Guns in the Camp* (1969), we learn, in the words of her husband Abu Saad:

> This woman [Umm Saad] has borne two sons who have grown up to become fidayeen. She provides the children for Palestine. (Kanafani, 2000: p131)

When Umm Saad is asked about her husband, she replies that he has been broken by years of defeat and poverty. But a new generation, inspired by fidayeen like Saad, are coming to the fore. These are the 'children of the camps' (awlad al-mukhayyamat), second, and today third and fourth, generation refugees fighting for their right to return. Kanafani's message is that the future belongs with the youth!

In the *Umm Saad* stories, there are two types of heroes. First there are Saad, his brother and the other fidayeen; armed fighters risking their lives for the cause. Second, there are people like Umm Saad, the 'ordinary' Palestinians in the camps, the community from which the fidayeen draw their members, their support and their strength. As Coffin notes:

The stories in *Umm Saad* attempt to demonstrate the transformative power of collective action...whilst [the fighters] role in the struggle for liberation is important, it cannot succeed without the active support of the general population. (Coffin, 1996: p114)

In *Returning to Haifa* (1969), Kanafani again conflates historical and narrative time to tell the story of a Palestinian couple, Said and Safiyya, over two episodes of their life: fleeing Haifa in April 1948 and returning for a visit in June 1967 after the Six Day War.

After the Israelis captured the West Bank from Jordan in 1967, they allowed Palestinians to travel into Palestine48 for visits but not to take up permanent residence. For many refugees, this was the first time they had been allowed to visit their former homes.

In the novel, Said and Safiyya travel from Ramallah to Haifa to visit their former home, which is now 'owned' by a Jewish couple, Iphrat and Miriam Koshen.

In the late 1940s and early 1950s, Jewish immigrants from Europe were encouraged to settle in Arab homes. The Israeli state used the Absentee Property Regulations of 1948 "to confiscate all Arab homes" and their (looted) contents (Krystall, 1998).

Kanafani tells us that Iphrat and Miriam fled to Palestine from Nazi Poland. They are not portrayed as Zionist zealots. Indeed, it is clear in the story that they have been misled by Zionist propaganda and are shocked by the reality of Israel.

In one passage, Miriam is horrified by the actions of "two young men from the Haganah" as they toss a dead Palestinian child onto the back of a truck. When Iphrat asks how she knew it was an Arab child, she replies:

Didn't you see how they threw it onto the truck, like a piece of wood? If it had been a Jewish child they would never have done that. (Kanafani, 2000: p169)

She draws a link between this child and her own younger brother, murdered in front of her by the Nazis as he returned home to tell her their father had been deported to Auschwitz.

Here Kanafani focuses on the horror of oppression and its consequences, wherever it occurs: the Holocaust in Europe and ethnic cleansing in Palestine. He does so by portraying the Israelis Miriam and Iphrat as sympathetic characters, perhaps the first Palestinian writer to do so in the post-Nakba period.

The novel is about abandonment and loss—generally, the Palestinians' loss of land and property in 1948, but specifically about Said and Safiyya's loss of their home, their property and their son, Khaldun. As the story unfolds, we learn that in the chaos and terror of the cleansing of Haifa in 1948, Safiyya and Said had left their infant son behind. They are returning to Haifa to look for Khaldun. When they arrive at their former home, it is remarkably unchanged. And they discover that Khaldun has been brought up by Miriam and Iphrat (who has since died) as their own. He is now known as Dov and is a soldier in the IDF.

The novel explores the complexities of the situation, made sharper by the events of the Six Day War. He is critical of the perspective that things 'should go back' to the way they were in 1948. This is best captured when Said asks: "What is a Homeland?" He goes on to ask:

Is it these two chairs that remained in this room for twenty years? The table? The peacock feathers? The picture of Jerusalem on the wall? The copper lock? The oak tree? The balcony? Khaldun? Our illusions about him? Fathers? Their sons? What is a homeland? (Kanafani, 2000: p184)

Instead, Kanafani asks us to consider the possibilities of Israeli Jews and Palestinians living together as part of a democratic, secular state.

The 'democratic, secular state' was the stated objective of the PFLP, and Fatah at the time. The PFLP believed it would take a people's revolution to obtain it, but it would be a state where Jews, Muslims, Christians and people of no faith could live with equal rights. Of course, any such state would mean the destruction of the racist Zionist entity, and for his writing and his leadership role within the PFLP, Kanafani was a wanted man.

Like *Men in the Sun*, and *All That's Left to You* before it, *Returning to Haifa* offers us a deeper understanding of the Palestinians' anguish and trauma. All three are shaped by betrayal, misfortune and injustice. All three portray the harsh reality of Palestinian refugee life. These three realist novellas highlight the injustices inflicted on the Palestinians and demand, from us within the wider global community, a just solution.

On 8 July 1972, Kanafani got in his car to travel to the shops. His niece Lamees got in the car with him. When he turned on the ignition the booby-trapped car exploded. Ghassan Kanafani, murdered by the Israelis, became a martyr for Palestine.

In his obituary in the *Lebanese Star*, he was described as "a commando who never fired a gun, whose weapon was the ballpoint pen, and his arena the newspaper pages".

He was a writer attuned to the political, social and human realities that characterise the lives of Palestinian refugees. He offered a voice for the refugee and a political perspective on the Nakba and its consequences. But his writings are not stuck in time. They continue to speak to us of the plight of refugees and the dispossessed across the Middle East. And the questions he poses, about refugee rights and the right of return, of the impact of Settler-Colonial conquest and the possibilities of establishing a secular, democratic Palestine, remain as relevant today as they were on that fateful day when the Israelis tried, but failed, to silence him forever.

Chapter 3
The 'present-absentee-alien' of Palestine48: Mahmoud Darwish (1942-1970)

IN ADDITION TO HIS CREATIVE WRITING, Ghassan Kanafani wrote an important overview of Palestinian literature within Palestine48. Resistance Literature in Occupied Palestine (1948-66) played a significant role in bringing the works of a number of Palestinian writers from inside Palestine48 to the wider diaspora and the wider world. Of those poets that Kanafani identified as being at the forefront of resistance literature, the most significant was Mahmoud Darwish.

Darwish was born on 13 March, 1942. He spent the first six years of his life on his family land in the village of Birweh in the Galilee. Birweh had more than 1,500 inhabitants, yet it was destroyed and cleansed by 'Brigade Seven', one of three Israeli brigades operating in the Galilee, in July 1948.

Brigade Seven were notorious, even by the standards of the Israeli Brigades, for their brutality. As Pappe notes:

> In many Palestinian oral histories that have now come to the fore, few brigade names appear. However, Brigade Seven is mentioned again and again, together with such adjectives as 'terrorists' and 'barbarous'. (Pappe, p158)

He would go on to publish more than 30 volumes of poetry and eight books of prose. At different points he was editor of the periodicals *Al-Ahram* (The Pyramid), *Al-Jadid* (The New), *Al-Fajr* (The Early Morning), *Shu'un Filistiniyya* (Palestinian Affairs) and *Al-Karmel*, named after the Carmel mountains outside Haifa.

His books of poetry sold in their hundreds of thousands, and

Mahmoud Darwish (1942-1970)

it was not uncommon for tens of thousands to attend his poetry readings. His popularity across the Arab world was akin to that of a Western pop or rock star.

He was a poet whose writings would universalise Palestine. His work, steeped in the Palestinian cause, brings together themes of agony and ecstasy, of pride, hope and despair, of horror, treachery, resilience, and resistance (Jayyusi, 1992: p60). He was the poet-spokesperson of his people who recorded the horrors inflicted on Palestine.

For example, in 'Poem of the Land', he commemorates Land Day. Land Day takes place on 30 March every year. It is a day of commemoration and marks the day when, in 1976, Israeli soldiers shot and killed six Palestinians (five of whom were schoolgirls) who were protesting the Israeli government's expropriation of thousands of donums of Palestinian land. Darwish dedicates the poem to the memory of those who were killed. It is quite a long poem within which Darwish explores the plight of Palestinians and the fact that they are 'victims of a map' and 'witnesses to massacre'. But it also movingly tells the young girls' stories:

> In the month of March
> in the year of the uprising
> earth told us her blood secrets
> In the month of March
> five girls at the door
> of the primary school
> Came past the violet
> came past the rifle
> burst into flames
> with the roses
> and thyme
> they opened
> the song of the soil
> and entered the earth
> the ultimate embrace.   (in Jayyusi, 1992: p145)

Darwish was first brought to the attention of the world by Kanafani. In *Resistance Literature in Occupied Palestine*, Kanafani argues that the Palestinians, like Darwish, who had been left inside 'Israel' after the Nakba, faced very particular problems. First, there was a significant change in the social structure within Palestine48.

Nearly three-quarters of the 200,000 Arabs who continued to live in their homeland were peasants. The cities were mostly evacuated either during the war or soon afterwards. This led to a shocking deterioration in Arab social conditions due to the fact that the cities had been the centres of both political and cultural effusion. (Kanafani, 1966: p3)

Second, the Nakba brought the forced exile of a whole generation of writers and men and women of culture. Those living under direct occupation, therefore, did not have a layer of intellectuals who could reflect their suffering in their writing and creative productions. Further, as Kanafani noted, those left inside Palestine48 were cut off from broader Arabic culture because of the effective two-way blockade between Israel and the surrounding Arab countries. As Elmessiri suggests:

Those who stayed in occupied Palestine...were left without intellectual leadership, separated from the rest of Arab culture, and subject to a variety of oppressive laws and regulations... A systematic policy of fighting Arab culture and history was implemented by the Israeli authorities. (Elmessiri, 1981: p77)

We need to be careful here!

The point Kanafani was making was that the population left inside Palestine48 were drawn from the poorest and less educated sectors of Palestinian society. But we should not assume that this meant workers and peasants had no culture or were incapable of cultural production. Indeed, the development of resistance literature inside Palestine48 grew out of oral traditions of poetic transmission that have deep roots in Arab society.

Third, the (now mainly) rural Arab society inside Palestine48 was subjected to significant repression. There were limits on Palestinians' political rights to organise and on their freedom of expression. Palestinian cultural life was also under immense pressure. For example, post-Nakba and up until the 1960s, there was not a single public library in any of the Palestinian towns or villages within Palestine48.

Palestinian writers faced immense difficulties publishing and performing their works because of pronounced censorship. This included a virtual ban on Arabic journals and magazines. Mattawa notes that between 1948 and 1967, only 64 books were published in Arabic and some of these were published by Arabic speaking Zionists from the Mizrahi (ie the Jewish Arab) community (Mattawa, 2014: p19).

The Israeli state were happy to use British Mandate emergency regulations against Arabs. Ashrawi notes that it was almost impossible to predict what might be censored because:

> it is difficult to predict the whims of the censor. Anything which might threaten 'the security of the state' is forbidden, but this is quite fluid since, according to the emergency laws, thinking thoughts harmful to the state is a legally punishable offence...the word 'Palestine' was considered threatening enough to be censored. (Ashrawi, 1978: p79)

Ziad, in the introduction to his anthology of previously censored poems Prisoners of Freedom, notes that the 'overly sensitive' Israeli authorities even tried to stop Arabs from singing!

Yet against this background, Kanafani identified the growth of resistance literature, in particular the growth of popular poetry that expressed the hopes, fears, anxieties and rebelliousness of the Arab population inside Palestine48. As Pappe notes:

> What political activists did not dare express, poets sang with force. Poetry was the one mediums through which the daily events of love and hate, birth and death, marriage and family could be intertwined with the political issues of land confiscation and state oppression. (Pappe, 2006: p157)

According to Jayyusi, in the Arab world:

> poetry is the main vehicle for expressing the emotional experience of a people, and for revealing their deeper

consciousness of the world, [as such, it can]...bring the reader into a more intimate knowledge of other people's actual life situations. (Jayyusi, 1987: p12)

Poets began to appear and perform at Palestinian festivities. Marriages, festivals and, especially, funerals became places where poets would recite political works. What Kanafani calls the poets vernacular form, shorter lines, the use of everyday images, the emphasis on the collective experiences of ordinary people, appealed to Arabs within Palestine48. The poems were steeped in the principles of adab al-iltizam. They were easier to relate to and understand, to learn and to recite.

And because the poems could not be easily published, they became performative pieces.

Poetry occupies a special place in Arab cultural traditions. According to Abdullah al-Udhari "poetry has been the mass art form of the Arab language...ever since pre-Islamic days". He continues:

Through the centuries of classical Arab civilisation in the Middle Ages, the long years of Arab decline, and into the decades of confrontation with European culture in the twentieth century, the poets have never lost their place of esteem. (al-Udhari, 2005: p7)

As an art form, it has had a significant role to play throughout history, telling stories of Arab victories and defeats. Peled suggests that "poetry was always considered a means of recording history and shaping it", with the poet:

expected to declare the attitude of society to everything that affected it, to guide it and eternalise its achievements. Poetry was meant to be heard in public rather than read in private. (Peled, 1982: p155)

Arabic poetry has always been involved in political struggles and in public engagement. It has also, historically, been performative. This performative aspect allowed poets wide audiences at a time when the majority of the population were illiterate or had only basic reading and writing skills. The performance element helped people to memorise the poems and repeat them in various settings.

Committing often long texts to memory was also embedded within Islamic culture as a sign of devotion and virtue and a means of passing the Quran from generation to generation. Memorising and repeating long poems, therefore, reflected aspects of the Islamic Haafiz tradition.

It remains the case today that poets have a greater impact on Arab culture than novelists. Across the region, in towns and villages, poets can still draw large audiences for public readings of their works.

Palestinian poets:

> even as they were being harassed and at times terrorised in Israel, even as they were experiencing the pains of exile outside their homeland, still participated in a living historical process that helped them maintain a sense of belonging, thereby over-coming the deep sense of alienation resulting from dislocation, dispersion and oppression. The traditions of resistance poetry were kept alive among the Palestinians in Israel, both through a few smuggled books that found their way from one reader to another, and through oral poetry recited during festivities and other occasions. (Elmessiri, 1981: p78)

The resistance poets combined elements of the traditional, such as harking back to the role of the poet as commentator on social events, with the new, utilising modernist poetic forms that appealed to a younger generation and which were a direct call to political action.

Mahmoud Darwish was a central figure in the developing movement. His poetry extols the virtues of resilience and resistance. It celebrates Palestine as both place and political entity. It embraces the nation as a means of galvanising people to join the struggle for liberation.

Darwish's expulsion and exile would be a life-defining event. He would never forget the last scenes of his village set on fire and obliterated, nor how he and his family had to flee in the middle of the night.

In one of his early poems, 'The Adam of Two Edens', he remembers that night's terrors and addresses his mother:

Do you remember our migration route to Lebanon?
When you forgot me in a sack of bread (it was a wheat bread)
I kept quiet so as not to wake the guards.
The scent of morning dew lifted me onto your shoulders.
O you gazelle that lost both house and mate.

(in Ghannam & El-Zein, 2009: p6)

Returning to the displacement in one of his later poems, 'Memory for Forgetfulness', he writes:

I became a poet who searches for the child that was in him, the child that he left somewhere and forgot. The poet grew up but he does not allow the forgotten child to grow. (Darwish, 1995: p82)

Commenting on these words in an interview in 1996 he argued:

In my situation, there are no essential differences between the story of my childhood and the story of my homeland. The rupture that occurred in my personal life also befell my homeland. Childhood was taken from me at the same time as my home. There is a parallelism and a unity in the tragic aspect of the matter. In 1948, when this great rapture of ours took place, I jumped from the bed of childhood onto the path of exile. I was six. My entire world turned upside down and childhood froze in place, it didn't go with me. The question is whether it's possible to restore the childhood that was taken by restoring the land that was taken, and that's a poetic quest that gives rhythm to the poem itself. Finding the child Mahmoud Darwish who once was is possible only in the poem. Not in life. (Yeshurun, 2012: p48)

As Birweh was raised to the ground, the Darwish family, like so many others, fled. At first, they went to Lebanon where they lived in a refugee camp. But, in 1949, they moved back across the border. Initially they stayed in Dayr-al-Asad before moving to al-Jadeeda, near to where Birweh had been. In an interview in 1969 with the Israeli Communist newspaper *Zo Hederekh* he said:

> All that had happened was that the refugee had exchanged his old address for a new one. I had been a refugee in Lebanon, and now I was a refugee in my own country. (in 'Victims of a Map', p10)

Birweh itself had been wiped off the map. In 1949 the village land was taken over by a Kibbutz.

In the 1950s, 60s and 70s, many on the left internationally saw Kibbutzim as something progressive, a form of 'socialism in action'.

The first Kibbutz was established in Palestine in 1909. It was founded upon utopian socialist ideals. People worked the land, all money and assets were commonly owned and collectively managed. People ate together in communal canteens, wore the same clothing, used communal laundries and had shared responsibilities for child-rearing, education and social services.

But there was a fundamental flaw: the Kibbutz movement was tied to the colonial-settlement project. Kibbutzim were established on Arab lands and local populations were consequently displaced. During and after the Nakba, Kibbutzim played a role in the expansion, and defence, of Israel's borders. Kibbutzim were often built along Israel's borders as part of Israel's defensive lines. Such was the case with the Kibbutz built on Birweh's land.

The deep sense of loss at the eradication of his village is captured by Darwish in his poem 'Standing Before the Ruins of Al-Birweh'. In the poem, Darwish tells us that he treads "lightly on the earth's skin/so as not to wake the dead", establishing his ancestral connection with the land. Because his return is so painful, he "shut[s] the door to my emotions to become my other" and then invokes two persona—one a tourist, one a journalist—to debate with him the fate of his land:

> Halt my two companions!
> Let us experience this place our own way:
> Here, a sky fell on a stone and bled it
> so that anemones would bloom in the spring

(Where is my song now?)
Here the gazelle broke the glass of my window
so that I would follow it
(So where is my song now?)
Here, the magical morning butterflies carried the path to my
school
(So where is my song now?)
Here I saddled a horse to fly to my stars
(So where is my song now?)

Darwish the poet-speaker now tells us that "he didn't grow up
and so did not go to exile" and that his father is "building my
tomorrow with his two hands".

But the journalist interrupts. The area has been modernised
with roads and factories; doesn't he see the progress?

Do you see that dairy factory behind that strong pine tree?
I say: No, I only see the gazelle at the window
He says: What about the modern roads on the rubble of
houses?
I say: No, I don't see them
I only see the garden under them
and I see the cobweb
He says: Dry your two tears with a handful of fresh grass
I say: That is my other crying over my past
                    (in Alshaer, 2019: pp53/54)

Defenders of Israel often invoke the claim that, whatever Israel
may have done in the past, it has brought economic development
and wealth to the country. Darwish's focus on the human cost
of displacement and the very real sense of loss that comes from
imposed exile punctures any such apologia. Further, as one reads
Darwish's poem, one cannot help but think of others such as the
First Peoples of Australia, New Zealand and the Americas whose
lives have been destroyed by the rampant 'progress' of capitalism
and colonialism, giving us modern states that were, as Marx noted,
born "dripping from head to toe, from every pore, with blood and
dirt" (Marx, 1867).

Mahmoud Darwish (1942-1970)

Because of their forced exile, the Darwish family were refugees within the new Israeli state borders, classified by the Israelis as 'present-absentee aliens'. According to the Israelis:

> The Palestinians who left were considered absent, and the Palestinians who stayed...were considered prisoners. Those who left and returned to find their houses destroyed were given the status of 'present-absent'—a new expression in language. (Ghannam & El-Zein, 2009: p2)

This designation meant Darwish was always an outsider. He was never allowed to become an Israeli citizen. In *Journal of an Ordinary Grief* (1973), Darwish describes his situation:

> You want to travel to Greece? You ask for a passport, but you discover you're not a citizen because your father or one of your relatives had fled with you during the Palestine War. You were a child. And you discover that any Arab who had left his country during that period and had stolen back in had lost his right to citizenship.

> You despair of the passport and ask for a laissez-passer. You find out you're not a resident of Israel because you have no certificate of residence. You think it's a joke and rush to tell your lawyer friend: "Here I'm not a citizen, and I'm not a resident. Then where and who am I? "You're surprised to find the law is on their side, and you must prove you exist. You ask the Ministry of the Interior, "Am I here, or am I absent? Give me an expert in philosophy, so that I can prove to him I exist." Then you realise that philosophically you exist but legally you do not. (Darwish, 2010: p66)

He attended Arab schools, but the teachers (many of whom were Jewish) had to hide him when Israeli education officers arrived. The curriculum was 'limited' and made no reference to Arab, and certainly not Palestinian history, nationality or culture. When he completed high school, he was not allowed to go to an Israeli university.

The high school curriculum prioritised Jewish history and

culture, and under the guidance of one of his favourite teachers, this sparked Darwish's long-term interest and engagement with Jewish literature and the Torah. He would regularly use Jewish prophets, psalms and stories, the tales of the suffering of the Jewish Diaspora, to shed light on the Palestinians' struggles.

When he started writing poetry, there were very few outlets to publish in Arabic. However, gradually Arab writers managed to publish their works.

> Israeli attempts to suppress...[Arab] literature did not succeed... and were gradually enfeebled by the perseverance of the politically committed poets and writers. (Ashrawi, 1978: p78)

One political space which brought Arab and Israeli activists together and enabled Arab writers to publish in their own language, was within the structures of the Israeli Communist Party.

The Communist Party was viewed as an 'Israeli' organisation by the Israeli state. As such it could publish in Arabic for no other reason than this would allow Mizrahi Jews to publish in their own language. Their newspaper *al-Ittihad* (Unity) and monthly magazine *al-Jadid* (The New) offered two of the very few outlets for Palestinian writers to publish in Arabic, something that would attract Darwish in his early career.

Several Arab intellectuals from within Palestine48 coalesced around the Communist Party. As Darwish was drawn into the orbit of the Party which he joined in 1961, he came into contact with a number of Palestinian activist writers. Three were particularly significant: Emile Habiby, Tawfiq Ziad and Samih al-Qasim.

Habiby, Ziad and al-Qasim were all born in Mandate Palestine, and each lived through the Nakba. All three continued to live in Palestine48 after the catastrophe, and each suffered under repressive, military laws and regulations in the 1950s and 1960s. However, unlike Darwish, each obtained Israeli citizenship.

Emile Habiby (1922-1996) is recognised as one the great writers on the Arab experience inside Palestine48. He was born in Haifa at the start of the British Mandate. Habiby and his family stayed in Haifa during and after the Nakba.

He was a member of the Palestine Communist Party during the Mandate era and became the secretary of the organisation in 1943. As a loyal Communist, he supported the UN proposals for the partition of Palestine. With the formation of Israel, he helped set up the Israeli Communist Party (Maki) though, in 1965, he split from the party to help set up the 'new' communist party (Rakah). The split was essentially between those (overwhelmingly Jewish) members who wanted to defend Israel's right to exist (and stayed in Maki) and those (overwhelmingly Arab) who took an anti-Zionist position (and set up Rakah). Habiby was elected to the Israeli Parliament (the Knesset) between 1951-1959 and from 1962-1972.

Habiby set up the paper *Al-Ittihad* (Unity) in 1944 which was shut down briefly by the British in 1948 and then at intervals by the Israelis. He continued to edit it until 1989. Habiby used the paper to write about all manner of social and political issues.

As a writer of fiction, Habiby came to prominence across the Arab world in the aftermath of the 1967 War, most notably through his collection of short stories *Stories of the Six Days* (1969). This was followed by his Palestinian epic, *The Secret Life of Saeed the Pessoptimist* (1974).

Habiby's novels can be difficult to follow. They are a mélange of realism and fantasy, of comedy and tragedy, and of history and satire.

The Secret a Life of Saeed the Pessoptimist, Habiby employs satire and bitter humour, to tell the story of Palestinians inside Israel, from 1948 to just after the six-day war of 1967.

In the novel, Saeed is a comic hero, who tells the story of his life in the form of a letter to a friend. He writes the letter from outer space after being saved by an extraterrestrial. Now safe, Saeed tells his story of terror and heroism, aggression and resistance, individual treason and community loyalty. This is the story of a life constantly lived on the point of crisis. It is a novel which veers between hope and horror and between pessimism and optimism (and it is from this mix that the portmanteau word 'Pessoptimist' is formed).

Edward Said described the novel as:

A carnivalesque explosion of parody and theatrical farce, continuously surprising, shocking, unpredictable. It makes no concessions at all to any of the standard fictional conventions... It is as if the Palestinian situation...produces a wildly erratic and free-wheeling version of the picaresque novel. (Said, 2000: p321/322)

In *Saraya, The Ogre's Daughter* (1990) Habiby combines folk tales, political commentary, allegory, and memoir to consider Palestine's past. The story is set in the former village of Al-Zeeb, north of Acre and it is themed around tracing and discovering the shifting identities of an apparition: Saraya. This is a device for Habiby to recollect the 'lost' Haifa of his youth, and the ruined landscape of Palestine.

The poet Tawfiq Ziad (1929-1994) moved in similar circles. Ziad was known for his 'poetry of protest' and trained and studied in the USSR. He saw himself as part of a global, anti-imperialist struggle for social justice, and part of a movement of the global poor and dispossessed. As such, he saw himself less as a specifically Palestinian writer. Nevertheless, he stood for elected office and became a member of the Knesset and Mayor of Nazareth (a position he held until his death in 1994).

His poem/song, 'Unadikum' is often played and sung on Nakba Day (15 May). *Unadikum* means 'I call to you' and is a great Palestinian nationalist anthem:

I call to you
I clasp your hands
And I kiss the earth beneath your feet
And I say unto you: I sacrifice myself for you
And dedicate the light of my eyes to you
And the warmth of the heart, I give you ...
The tragedy is that I live
My share of tragedy is that of yours
I call to you
I clasp your hands

Mahmoud Darwish (1942-1970)

I have not spared myself for my homeland or underestimated
the power of my hands

I have stood in the face of my oppressors

Orphaned, naked and barefooted...

I have carried my blood on my palm

And I have not lowered my flag

And I have protected the green grass above the tombs of my
ancestors

I call to you, I call to you   (Alshaer, 2019: p66)

Samih al-Qasim (1939-2014) was a poet from the Palestinian
Druze community. He came from Rameh, in the Upper Galilee.
He went to school in Nazareth and claims that his first school
child's memories were of the Nakba. Writing in 1970 he asserted:

> While I was still at primary school the Palestinian tragedy
> occurred. I regard that date as the date of my birth, because
> the first images I can remember are of the 1948 events. My
> thoughts and images spring from the number 48. (Adonis et al,
> 2005: p50)

He was imprisoned several times, including, in 1960, for refusing
to join the Israeli army (as those from the Druze community are
expected to do). In an interview in the journal *Index*, in December
1983, he was asked why he stayed in Israel. He responded by
drawing on Shakespeare's *Julius Caesar*:

> You know that part of Brutus's speech in which he says: "If
> then that friend demand why Brutus rose against Caesar, this
> is my answer: not that I love Caesar less, but that I love Rome
> more". I have chosen to remain in my country not because I
> love myself less, but because I love my homeland more... [and
> so]...I haven't visited Baghdad or any Arab city. But I follow
> everything that goes on in those cities from my great prison.

That idea of Israel being a prison appears in one of his short
poems 'End of a Discussion With a Prison Guard':

> Through the eyehole of this little cell of mine
> I can see the trees all smiling at me,
> The rooftops crowded with my family,

The windows breaking into tears for me.
And prayers for me.
Through the eyehole of this little cell of mine
I see your bigger cell just fine.

(Alshaer, 2019: p55)

Like so many, his politics were initially pan-Arabist, but the war of 1967, as noted above, was a major turning point in Palestinian politics. The heavy defeat of the Arab armies in the Six Day War produced a shift in emphasis. Instead of hoping liberation would come via armed intervention from an Arab army, Palestinians looked increasingly towards their own self-organisation and self-emancipation. For al-Qasim, it meant joining the Israeli Communist Party. At various points he edited the Communist journal *al-Ittihad*, the cultural magazine *al-Jadid*, and he was the long-time editor-in-chief of the Israeli Arab paper *Kul al-Arab* (All Arabs).

Habiby, Ziad and al-Qasim all represent a vibrant Palestinian presence inside Palestine48. That aspect of the Palestinian experience is often forgotten as those in the solidarity movement focus on the refugee communities in Gaza, the West Bank or in the camps across the Arab world.

Habiby, Ziad and al-Qasim were part of a welcoming milieu within which Darwish would develop and flourish as a committed artist.

Darwish's poetry draws on the strong oral traditions of Palestinian culture, where catchy expressions, verses and rhythms are retained and passed between people. Poetry is the most popular genre within Palestinian literature, and it is viewed as an expression of national solidarity and political consciousness. Over the years, several of his poems have been put to music and recorded, and many can be found on YouTube.

Performance poetry would also bring Darwish to the attention of the Israeli state.

One of his first poetic performances was when he was still at school. When he was in the Eighth Form, the Israeli authorities forced Arab schools to participate in the annual celebrations of

Israel's Independence Day. Darwish was chosen to represent the school and he took part in the village celebrations.

For the occasion, he wrote and recited his poem 'My Brother, the Hebrew' (1958). The poem compared his life and his educational opportunities with that of a Jewish youngster of the same age. It is written as an emotional cry from an Arab boy to his Jewish friend:

You play in the sun as you please and have your toys.
I can't.
You have a house,
I have none.
You have celebrations,
I have none.
Why can't we play together?   (in Padel, 2009: p16)

The following day, he was called to the Military Governor's office. There he was told that, as an Arab in Israel, he should not compare himself with a Jew, that he should not even dream of possessing what a Jew may have. The Governor ended his warning, "If you continue writing such things, I will stop your father working in the quarry" (al-Udhari, 1984).

During his time living in Palestine48, Darwish would serve five periods of imprisonment mainly for publishing, performing or travelling to perform poetry. In addition, he would spend significant spells under house arrest (Mattawa, 2014: pp15 & 24).

But such harassment brought with it a realisation that his poetry was, in his words, "a threat to the sword". In other words, he gained strength from recognising that his poetry was viewed by the occupation forces as a challenge to their authority.

One of his earliest collections, *Birds Without Wings* (1961), encapsulates the feelings of isolation and the lack of freedom Palestinians 'imprisoned' within Palestine48 suffered. Up until 1966, Palestinians living within the borders of Israel were subject to military rule and a complex set of emergency regulations. This even included significant restrictions to freedom of movement: it was necessary to obtain a permit to travel from village to village within Palestine48, so even meeting family members in neighbouring villages became difficult.

At this stage, the Communist Party were fighting for Palestinian equality within Israel, demanding equal treatment and freedom of speech, political participation and movement.

Darwish's early poetry sets out to assert the Arab presence in Palestine, to collectivise the experiences of oppression and establish the Palestinian, individually and collectively, as a political subject.

As Mattawa notes of this early period:

> Darwish focus[es] on public concerns that all citizens share. The impact of colonial oppression...the struggle over land, racial equality, national self-determination and social justice. (Mattawa, 2014: p44)

83

These are both public and private issues. Every aspect of life for Palestinians within Palestine48 is affected and shaped by the consequences of colonial settlement.

These themes are covered in some of his early poems. Let's take four examples: 'To My Mother', 'A Lover from Palestine', 'And He Returned in a Shroud' and 'Identity Card'.

'To My Mother' was written when Darwish was in prison. It is a relatively short poem about home, family security and the naturalness of small things, like his mother's bread or coffee. But it works on two levels: on the one hand it is a celebration of home and family, but on the other it identifies Palestine as 'the mother' and the home comforts are those of his native land.

Written in the form of a letter, he starts by conveying his longing for home comforts and security:

> I yearn for my mother's bread,
> My mother's coffee,
> Mother's brushing touch.

These simple things are important during difficult times:

> ...I so cherish life
> Because if I died
> My mother's tears would shame me.

In the second stanza, the poet-speaker asks for motherly protection in an uncertain future, to look after him whether he should come home either dead or alive: "Take me, if I come back one day/As a scarf for your eyelashes/And cover my bones with grass".

Whilst the last stanza reflects happier times of his childhood, in his home, in the bosom of his family.

Give me back the stars of childhood
That I may chart the homeward quest
Back with the migrant birds,
Back to your awaiting nest.   (Darwish, 2011)

The poem has an image, perhaps idealised, of home and family life in Palestine at a happier time before exile, occupation and imprisonment.

In Darwish's poetry, memories of the lost homeland are often captured by minute details of aspects of pre-Nakba life: dogs barking, roaming gazelle, birds, plants, aspects of the harvest and even the moon. It is remembered by reference to its mountains and plains, its sea and its shores, its lakes, and rivers. As Nashef points out:

Darwish...reconnects with the homeland through tangible objects. References to pebbles and rocks [for example] are prevalent in Darwish's work, and they represent the poet's attempt at rendering the abstract tangible through his use of metaphor. (Nashef, 2016)

Darwish's great strength was the way he managed to describe mundane events and uncover his innermost feelings through words juxtaposed in the most idiosyncratic of contexts, creating fascinating new images. The symbols, metaphors and style in his poetry are carefully chosen. He wrote poems, at least in his early days, that could be easily understood, and as a result many of his poems have been turned into songs sung by some of the Arab world's leading musicians (many of which you can find on YouTube).

The popularity of 'To My Mother' is not just about its image of 'simpler times' before the Nakba, or its allusion to the homeland. It also speaks to those families who have members in prison and the dream of simpler things in the bosom of one's home.

Since the Naksa of 1967, it is estimated that close to one million Palestinians have been arrested by Israeli state forces. According to the prisoner's rights organisation Ad-Dameer, as of March 2019 there were 5,450 Palestinian political prisoners scattered across 22 prisons in Israel and the occupied West Bank; 497 being held under 'administrative detention', which allows for their indefinite detention without charge or trial. The dream of home and simple things like a mother's coffee, bread and protection continue to speak to those who face time as political prisoners in Israeli gaols.

In 'A Lover from Palestine', Darwish seems to write a non-political, traditional poem apparently about an unrequited love. He describes his love:

> Your lips are honey and your hand
> a cup of wine
> for others...
> And the silk of your breast, your basil, your dew
> are a comfortable bed
> for others...
>
> And I am the sleepless one lying by your black walls;
> I am the sand's thirst, the shiver of nerves in firesides.
> Who can shut the door before me?
> What tyrant, what fiend?
> I will love your nectar
> even though it is poured in the cups of others
> (in Mattawa, 2014: p47)

But this is not a simple poem of rejected love.

At the same time, Darwish wrote the poem 'To the Reader'. Here he tells us he would, ideally, like to be able to write poetry that spoke of universal themes like love but that this is not possible. He tells us he has no choice but to express anger at what his people face:

Black tulips in my heart,
flames on my lips:
from which forest did you come to me,
all you crosses of anger?
I have recognized my grief
and embraced wandering and hunger.
Anger lives in my hands,
anger lives in my mouth
and in the blood of my arteries swims anger.

O reader,
don't expect whispers from me,
or words of ecstasy;
this is my suffering!
A foolish blow in the sand
and another in the clouds.
Anger is all I am –
anger, the tinder
of fire.   (in Asfour, 1988)

He tells us not to expect 'whispers' or 'words of ecstasy'. He cannot write simple love poems, but is forced by circumstances to write poems that express Palestinian anger and that will hopefully generate 'fire' in the form of political resistance. This being so, what is 'A Lover From Palestine' about?

The key phrase that he repeats is 'for others'. The poem is about his love for his country, now taken (not given) by others (the 'tyrants and fiends'). And his resilience to stay (unquenchable, like the sand's thirst) by the 'black walls' (those that have been charred by bombs or fire) to reclaim his lost love. As Ahmed et al note:

[in this poem] Darwish transforms the occupied land of
Palestine into the pure beloved whose images constitute the
poet's sense of attachment. The various natural features of
Palestine—it's flowers, birds, animals, water, wind, storms and
trees amongst so many others—are closely linked with human
organs to evoke interdependence. In these images, depicted
from the Palestinian environment, nature is associated with

man in his resistance. (Ahmed et al, 2012:p13)

'A Lover From Palestine' is, then, a resistance poem. It is about love of one's country in the face of occupation and oppression. And to his audience, as he performed his poem, this sense of love for a lost land and home is clear.

Similarly, Darwish collectivises the consequences of death and oppression. The motif of death is a recurring one in his poetry, and its meaning changes over time: it appears as glorification or as martyrdom or as tragedy (Hamzah, 2014).

In the poem 'And He Returned in a Shroud', Darwish tells the story of a young man who left home and returned wrapped in a shroud. We are not told why he left (through choice, economic compulsion, expulsion, arrest?) and though the poet-speaker makes it clear he knows this young man well, he chooses not to name him; if we name him, he will just be another on a long list of the dead. So, he beseeches us to keep our memories, and his name, in our heart:

> They talk in our country
> They talk with grief
> About my friend who went away
> And returned in a shroud.
>
> His name was...
> Don't say his name
> Leave it in our hearts
> Don't let his name
> Be lost like ashes in the wind
> Let it be a bleeding wound
> Unknown even to its bandage.
>
> Friends and orphans! I'm afraid!
> I'm afraid it will be lost
> In files of names
> And storms of winter
> I'm afraid our own wounds
> Will fall asleep.

By not naming the victim, he becomes someone we can all relate

Mahmoud Darwish (1942-1970)

to. To Palestinian families, this could be a father, a son, a brother.

Darwish similarly refuses to name the victims in his poem 'Victim Number 18', a poem about the 1956 massacre by Israeli border guards of 48 men, women, and children in the village of Kfar Qasim within Palestine48. It is only at the end of the poem that we discover that the poet-narrator is the unnamed 18th victim.

In the second and third passages of 'And He Returned in a Shroud', Darwish establishes the man's youthful innocence. He is 'the age of a bud', he was 'immune to insomnia', he had 'never kissed a woman, except twice'. The poem makes clear, he didn't deserve to die. He was young, with his life ahead of him and his loss is deeply felt.

In the fourth passage, he turns to address the young man's mother. He recognises and notes her sorrow but tells her not to use all her tears up (don't pull them 'by the root'). This is because, for Palestinians, death is never far away:

For tomorrow his father may die...or his brother
Or I, his friend

Finally, in the fifth section we learn that he died a violent death.

They speak a great deal in our country
About my friend,
The fires of lead on his cheeks
His chest...his face.
Don't explain things!
I saw his wound,
I stared deep into his horizons...
My heart goes out to our children
And each mother that embraces a deathbed

The poem ends with a call to arms:
'when will our men wake up!"
(in Mattawa, 2014)

'And He Returned in a Shroud' embodies many of the themes of adab al-iltizam; accessibly written, it uses common language, draws on and generalises from common experience and includes a political call to arms.

The poem continues to speak to the Palestinian experience.

In March 2018, Palestinians in Gaza began protesting for their right to return to their homes in Palestine48 and against the twelve-year siege of Gaza. The protests originated in a Facebook post by Palestinian journalist and poet Ahmed Abu Artema. Abu Artema called on Palestinian refugees to gather peacefully near the fence with Israel and attempt to return to their pre-1948 homes. His call led to weekly Friday protests, which became known as the "Great March of Return" rallies.

Every Friday Palestinians marched, peacefully, to the 'Separation Wall' where they were met with horrendous levels of violence. By March 2019, according to Gaza's Health Ministry, Israeli snipers had killed 266 people and injured almost 30,000 others (Fayyed, 2019).

B'Tselem argue:

Israel has implemented an unlawful open-fire policy towards Palestinians protesting near the Gaza perimeter fence, which permits live fire at unarmed protestors who pose no danger to anyone. (B'Tselem, 2019)

The dead include children, adults (both young and old), men and women, medics, teachers, nurses, journalists and students, each 'returned home in a shroud', each had the 'fire of lead on their cheeks or chest'.

For Palestinians, death or injury at the hands of Israeli forces is not something distant or abstract. It is part of daily life. Half a century after it was written, the poem continues to speak for those who meet a violent end at the hands of the murderous Israeli forces.

Similarly, 'Identity Card' continues to speak to Palestinian realities.

'Identity Card' is one of Darwish's most famous poems. We touched upon it in the introduction. It appeared in 1964 in the collection *Olive Leaves*, written when Darwish was 23.

The poem was inspired by his experience whilst under house

arrest in the early-1960s in Haifa. He had been charged with publishing a poem and the judge gave him probation with some conditions attached. He was forbidden to leave his house after sunset and he had to report daily to the local police station.

In 'Memory for Forgetfulness' (2013/1986) Darwish recalled that he was so angry with this daily humiliation that on one occasion he shouted at the officer in Hebrew: "Write it down: I am Arab".

At the time, the Israeli state refused to acknowledge that Palestine or Palestinians existed. Palestinians living within Palestine48 were simply referred to as Arabs.

The poem's popularity is rooted in the fact that it gives expression to a common experience: the ritual humiliation suffered by Palestinians at checkpoints when stopped by soldiers or police as they go about their daily activities, or when engaging in any way with the multi-layered Israeli bureaucracy.

To emphasise the point, across the West Bank there are a series of permanent checkpoints, supplemented every day by 'flying checkpoints' or roadblocks where soldiers stop traffic and monitor Palestinian movement.

In July 2018, the UN Office for the Coordination of Humanitarian Affairs noted that there were: "705 permanent obstacles across the West Bank restricting or controlling Palestinian vehicular, and in some cases pedestrian, movement". This number included:

140 [permanent] checkpoints...but only 64 of them are permanently staffed with security forces... The other 76 (partial) checkpoints are either occasionally staffed or have security personnel located in a tower rather than on the ground.
Excluded from these figures are eight checkpoints located on the Green (1949 Armistice) Line. Between January 2017 and the end of July 2018, Israeli forces employed an additional 4,924 ad-hoc "flying" checkpoints, or nearly 60 a week. These involve the deployment of Israeli forces for several hours on a given road for the purpose of stopping and checking Palestinian drivers and vehicles, but without any permanent physical

infrastructure on the ground. (UNOCHA, 2018)

All Palestinians from the age of sixteen carry identity cards within Palestine48, the West Bank and Gaza. These are colour-coded. The colouring differs depending on where the holder's family lives. They identify their religion and make it clear where they can and cannot travel and enter.

But the dispersal of Palestinian refugees in the diaspora means that Palestinians have a range of passports and IDs: for example, today Palestinians may hold, amongst others, Jordanian, Syrian, Kuwaiti, American, Canadian or Chilean passports, or they may have no ID at all. Indeed, within the same family it is possible that people will hold a range of passports and IDs, and these will all impact on their ability to access different parts of 'Israel' should they chose to visit.

Thus, every Palestinian has direct experience of the ritualised humiliation associated with scrutiny of one's ID card.

The assertion "Write it down! I am an Arab" is about Palestinians asserting their right to exist and their rights to the land. It is about defiance in the face of Israeli harassment. And it captures something of what Palestinians call 'samoud', literally 'steadfastness' but perhaps better understood as bloody-minded resilience and determination not to concede an inch to the occupier.

The poem is written in free verse. The speaker is an ordinary Palestinian, a worker. Its power lies partially in its stark language, uplifting tone and simple, direct images which endow the speaker with a kind of primal nobility. Read with that aspect of samoud to the fore, it becomes a brilliant piece that asserts Palestinian agency:

Write it down!
I am an Arab
employed with fellow workers at the quarry
I have eight children
I earn their bread,
clothes and books
out of these rocks.

Mahmoud Darwish (1942-1970)

I do not beg for charity at your doors.
Nor do I kneel
on your marble floor.
So does this anger you?

Write it down!
I am an Arab.
...
My father comes from the family of the plough
not from a privileged clan.
And my grandfather, a farmer,
not well-bred or well-born,
taught me how to read.
...
Write it down!
I am an Arab,
hair colour black, black as coal,
eyes brown.
Features:
an 'iqual on my head tied around a kaffiyah,
a hand solid as a stone
that scratches whoever touches it.
And my address:
a weaponless village, forgotten,
its streets too without names,
all its men are in the quarry or the fields.
Does this anger you?

And then the final verse, covered in the introduction, which
notes that the Israelis have stolen orchards and land and left
Palestinians with nothing. The verse ending with the words:

I do not hate people
nor do I steal.
But if I become hungry
I will eat my robber's flesh
Beware then, beware of my hunger
and my anger!

Darwish regularly performed 'Identity Card' to Palestinian audiences, but he refused to perform it for non-Palestinian audiences across the Middle East. For Darwish this was a poem specific to Palestinian realities, it was not a piece that spoke to a more general Arab nationalist sentiment.

Surprisingly, on 19 July 2016 'Identity Card' was read out on Israeli army radio, which caused uproar. Israeli media commentators and politicians denounced the poem and its recital.

Miri Regev, Minister of Culture and Sports, said she was terrified by the reading and attacked the Army Radio for including the poem in its programme. Defense Minister Avigdor Lieberman compared Darwish to Adolph Hitler. The newspaper *Israel Today* wrote that airing the poem was like broadcasting a programme to Israeli soldiers about Hitler's *Mein Kampf*, "because both have one aim: to destroy the Jews." (Hilmy, 2017)

Regev, Lieberman, *Israel Today* and other critics found it convenient to ignore the poem's background or context and the explicit assertion that "I do not hate people" just before its concluding warning to "the occupier".

Darwish, the resistance poet of Palestine48, was proud that his work represented "a challenge to the sword". Perhaps there is no better testament to Darwish than the fact that his poem, written in 1964 and read out in 2016, eight years after his death in 2008, was still seen as a challenge by those in power in Israel.

Whilst he lived in Palestine48, Darwish's poems were deeply affected by the political and cultural context within which he found himself. As Hamzah notes:

> During the 1960s Darwish's poetry can be said to have mainly carried a message which served the collective. The poet saw himself as a messenger whose function it was to report truthfully what was happening within his society. (Hamzah, 2014: p161)

However, by the late 1960s, Israeli harassment of Darwish pushed him to look at ways out. He had been imprisoned four times in the 1960s for publishing and performing his poems. In

1969 the Israelis arrested him and tried to link him to a resistance military action. There was no evidence, but Darwish recognised that being set up for terror charges could lead to a significant prison sentence.

In 1970 he was given permission to leave Israel as part of an Israeli Communist Party delegation to Moscow. He took the opportunity and decided to stay on in Russia with a Moscow University scholarship.

The following year he left Moscow but did not go back to Palestine48. Instead, he moved to Cairo to work as a journalist at the newspaper *al-Ahram* (The Pyramids).

Darwish's decision was not uniformly popular. Several people, including Kanafani and Habiby and many of his comrades in the Communist Party, denounced him for desertion. Reflecting on his decision, he said:

> It was the most difficult decision of my life... For 10 years I was not allowed to leave Haifa. After 1967 I was under house arrest... I was too young to see the balance between standing up to these conditions or finding an open sky for my little wings as a poet. I was seduced by adventure. But the final judgment has to come from what I did in exile. (Jaggi, 2002)

The move to exile marked a change in direction to both Darwish's artistic output and his political engagement. His early poems defined Palestinian existence, reasserting Palestinian identity within Palestine48 after the dispersal of the Nakba.

As we will see in the next chapter, the decision to leave for Egypt brought about a change in focus and brought him into closer contact with the leadership of the PLO.

Chapter 4

The wandering exile of the Palestinian Diaspora: Mahmoud Darwish (1970-2008)

WHEN DARWISH LEFT PALESTINE48 in 1970, he began to describe himself as a 'wandering exile' (www.mahmouddarwish.com). Over the next phase of his life, he spent time living in Russia, Egypt, Lebanon, Tunisia, Jordan, France and the West Bank.

At various points he wrote poems that captured something of the enforced nomadic existence he and many exiled Palestinians face in contrast to the highly regulated, 'imprisoned' existence facing those living in Palestine48.

In 'Athens Airport', Darwish introduces a fighter, a pregnant woman, a banker, an intellectual and a young married couple 'trapped' in Athens: "We have waited in Athens airport for years", they say.

The Greek airport was a hub for Palestinians moving from place to place. But where can they go? Where will they be welcomed? Why can't they go home?

In the poem, the fighter asks where should he go to fight? The pregnant woman asks where she can give birth? The married couple ask where they can go to consummate their relationship? The banker asks where he can invest his money?

Towards the end of the poem are two agonised questions: "What do they want from us?... O Athens airport, how many more years will this waiting take?" (Adonis et al, 2005: p37).

Similarly, in 'Diary of a Palestinian Wound' Darwish contrasts the suitcase of the traveller or holiday maker with that of the refugee:

My country is not a suitcase
I am not a traveller

The freedom afforded many of us to journey for work or holidays is not the same as the movement of exiles whose travels are limited or monitored, and who cannot return home. We may all store our belongings in a suitcase but the meaning associated with it are quite different.

Interestingly, after the Israeli siege of Beirut in August 1982 (see below), in the poem 'In Praise of the Lofty Shadow', he wrote 'My homeland is a suitcase' this time reflecting on his second significant, Israeli induced displacement when he was forced to leave Beirut (his home from 1973-1982) for Tunis.

When he left Russia in 1971, he moved to Egypt. Two years later, he was persuaded to move to Beirut to work for the PLO.

The PLO had relocated its base from Amman to Beirut in the aftermath of Black September 1970, when the Jordanian regime moved against the Palestinian fidayeen, concerned that their growing strength threatened the autocratic rule of King Hussain.

In Beirut, he became director of the PLO Centre of Palestine Studies, editor of *Shu'un Filastiniya* (Palestinian Affairs), and an Executive Committee member of the PLO. In Beirut, he moved into Yasser Arafat's orbit, often acting as his speech writer. Perhaps most notably he helped to write Arafat's speech to the UN General Assembly in November 1974, where Arafat, dressed in military uniform, gun-holster on his side and keffiyeh on his head, finished by saying:

> I come bearing an olive branch in one hand and a freedom fighter's gun in the other. Do not let the olive branch fall from my hand. (Arafat, 1974)

In 1988, alongside Edward Said, he wrote the Palestinian declaration of independence. The Declaration opens with the words, "Palestine, the land of the three monotheistic faiths...' This observes Jewish, Muslim and Christian connections with Palestine and goes on to note the historic injustice inflicted on the Palestinians through the Nakba, which has had the effect of denying Palestinians' right to self-determination. The

Declaration also recognises the legality of the UN Partition plan of 1947 and thus paves the way for the PLO to move towards acceptance of the two-state solution to the Palestinian question.

Darwish's role in writing the Declaration and various of Arafat's speeches indicate that he was becoming deeply embedded in the Palestinian political machinery.

Darwish's move from Palestine48 had brought a number of changes to his life.

He went from the restrictions of the 'internal prison' to a situation of relative 'freedom' of movement, certainly across the Arab world. Of course, this was still the 'freedom' of an exile who cannot return home.

From 'outsider' poet, fighting to be heard, he became one of the most celebrated poets in the diaspora and across the Middle East.

Instead of struggling to get published, or at least publishing in struggling Arabic publications in Palestine48, he began writing for some of the largest selling papers and journals in the Middle East.

Membership of the Israeli Communist Party, a small network on the periphery of anti-establishment politics within Palestine48, was replaced by membership and, indeed, leadership within the PLO. The PLO was, of course, the main Palestinian establishment organization, though one that was denigrated as a terrorist organisation by Israel and the main imperial powers.

All these changes would impact in various ways on his writing. The focus of his poetry moved from those who were 'left behind', reflecting his direct experience of life in Palestine48, to those who were part of the diasporas and those who were part of the resistance.

He joined the PLO after it had been through a period of ideological transition.

After their victory at Karameh in 1968, Fatah and the main Palestinian resistance organisations grew dramatically. According to Neff:

Never before had Palestinians stood and fought the Israel
Defense Forces to a standstill in such a large battle, nor had

they ever inflicted such casualties. Refugee camps throughout the Arab world hailed the rebirth of the Palestinian people and volunteers flocked to the guerrilla groups. Fatah reported that 5,000 volunteers applied to join within 48 hours of the battle. (Neff, 1988)

Hirst suggests that:

New recruits flocked to training camps [in Jordan]... The fighting forces of Fatah—some 300 before Karameh...had swollen to more than 30,000 two years later. (Hirst, 2003: p424)

And it was not just Palestinians who volunteered. An estimated 20,000 Egyptians and 1,500 Iraqis joined the various fidayeen factions (Hirst, 2003: p413).

The main Palestinian faction, Fatah, led by Arafat, was less ideological than the smaller more radical organisations such as the Popular Front for the Liberation of Palestine (PFLP) and the Democratic Front for the Liberation of Palestine (DFLP).

But in the late 1960s, Fatah came to the realisation that the guerrilla war could not develop if it was built upon the idea of vengeance and revenge for past grievances. Rather, the movement had to have a vision of an alternative future. This vision was encapsulated in the idea of the Democratic State of Palestine.

In some earlier iterations, for example some of Habash's statements within the early days of the Arab Nationalist Movement, there was a tendency to conflate Zionists with Jews. This reflected Zionist propaganda that insisted that all Jews were Zionists (Hirst, 2003: p418). But it also grew out of bitterness at the refugee experience of dispossession and expulsion in the Nakba.

However, the growth of the fidayeen, the political culture generated within the movement, and the engagement with other international liberation struggles led to significant political education and development. Significantly, a real distinction developed between understandings of Jews and Zionists within the fidayeen, and then more generally in Palestinian civil society.

In 1970, for example, the PLO produced a pamphlet *Towards a Democratic State in Palestine* (Rashid, 1970) which argued that Jews had suffered oppression and persecution at the hands of racists and Nazis and that many Jews had fled Europe to escape antisemitism. As such, they had faced many of the injustices now confronting Palestinians. It also argued that many Jewish migrants to Israel had been led to believe that the Palestinians had chosen to leave of their own free will. They were led to believe that it was necessary to fight to stop a massacre of Jewish people by Arab armies. It was, then, the Zionists (that is the ideologues, the powerful, the ruling oligarchs), who were the enemy not ordinary Jewish people.

The pamphlet was part of a move by the PLO to promote the Democratic State as their preferred solution to the crisis. As Walker and Gowers note:

> [Fatah] were now proposing to co-operate with those Jews who had been prepared to throw off the shackles of Zionism in building a completely new society. ...the idea of a free and democratic society in Palestine for all Palestinians including Muslims, Christians and Jews...became official PLO policy. (Walker & Gowers, 2003: p58)

This development was attractive to someone like Darwish, brought up inside Palestine48, a reader of Hebrew and with many Jewish friends and acquaintances. In 1971, in an interview in an Israeli magazine, he told readers that his poetry had gained an audience across the Arab world and that Arab readers of his poems were aware that his writing spoke of "the rights of Jews and Arabs to exist in Palestine" (in Mattawa, 2014: p62).

In some of his poems of the late 1960s, Darwish includes significant and strong Jewish characters. In 'A Soldier Dreams of White Lilies', Darwish tells of a story about the friendship of an Israeli soldier and Mahmoud, the narrator of the poem. The poem starts with a description of the soldier:

> He dreams of white lilies
> an olive branch
> and of her breast in evening bloom.

Mahmoud Darwish (1970-2008)

He dreams, he told me, of a bird,
a lemon blossom,
and he did not philosophise his dream.
He did not understand things
except in the way he felt them, smelled them.
He understood, he told me, that "the country"
is to drink my mother's coffee
To return home safely in the evening.

The poem starts by introducing a number of images common to Darwish's poetry: olive branch, lemon blossom, birds, all symbols he used previously to describe aspects of life and peace in pre-Nakba Palestine, and, as noted in the previous chapter, a 'mother's coffee', a common symbol of stability and home-life. Here, Darwish uses these common images to stress what we have in common; they convey aspects of our shared humanity. The poem goes on to talk about the soldier's mother's anxieties when he goes on duty and his first love. Again, themes which resonate across the Palestinian/Israeli divide.

But the poem also covers the soldier's role in killing Palestinians. Mahmoud asks his friend to 'describe one victim to me'. He responds:

"Like a tent, he fell on the gravel
and embraced the shattered planets.
There was a crown of blood on his wide brow,
his chest without medals,
because he was not good at killing,
maybe a farmer, or a labourer, or a travelling salesman.
Like a tent he fell on the gravel, and died.
His arms
stretched like two dry streams
and when I searched his pockets
for his name, I found two pictures,
one of his wife,
one of his little girl..."
– "were you sad" I asked. He answered, interrupting me,

– "Mahmoud, my friend,
...
soldiers commit a grave sin
when they fall sad. I was a machine there,
blowing rose-coloured fire
that turned space into a black bird"   (Darwish, 2012)

The poem begins by tracing the soldier's desire for peace and his love for 'ordinary things', which point to what we have in common. But whilst on duty and following orders, the soldier becomes part of an oppressive apparatus and acts brutally and with impunity; he becomes a 'machine' that blows out 'rose-coloured fire'.

The poem seems to suggest that it is not individuals that are the problem but the system and what it demands of people.

'Rita and the Rifle' again looks at the possibilities of love and affection developing between people from different communities. The poem tells the story of two lovers, a Jewish woman called Rita and the Palestinian narrator. Their love is intense and has lasted for two years. The narrator tells us:

...whoever knows Rita
Kneels and prays
To the divinity in those honey-coloured eyes.
And I kissed Rita
When she was young
...
Rita's name was a feast in my mouth
Rita's body was a wedding in my blood
And I was lost in Rita for two years
And for two years she slept on my arm
And we made promises

But the lovers' relationship is brought to a halt when Rita is given a rifle and conscripted into the IDF. Now:

Between Rita and my eyes
There is a rifle

The rifle and membership of the IDF change everything. The narrator makes the point repeatedly:

Ah, Rita
Between us there are a million sparrows and images
And many a rendezvous
Fired at by a rifle.
...
Ah, Rita!
What before this rifle could have turned my eyes from yours
Except a nap or two or honey-coloured clouds?
Between Rita and my eyes—
A rifle.

(Darwish, 2012b)

The explicit shift in Fatah's, and the PLO's, political goals, therefore, spoke to Darwish's own musings that coexistence was entirely possible and that the problem in Palestine was essentially political: the philosophy and practice of Zionism. In 'Rita and the Rifle' and 'A Soldier Dreams of White Lilies', the peaceful and human relations between Israeli and Palestinian are destroyed by the incorporation of Israelis, via conscription, into the IDF. It is the system of colonial settlement and oppression that is the barrier to peace.

In Lebanon Darwish came to be viewed as the official poet of the PLO. As such there were certain expectations placed upon him by his audience and from within the PLO. Reflecting on this period after he left Beirut, Darwish suggested he felt a conflict between Darwish the poet and Darwish the politician.

Barbara Harlow (1987), in her review of resistance literatures from across the globe, describes resistance poetry as a form of literature that accompanies armed struggle, that is composed on or near the battlefield and which commemorates, or lionises, the fighters and the casualties. During his time in Lebanon Darwish's poetry moves more explicitly in this direction, take two examples: 'In Going to the World: A stranger to the world' and 'Ahmad al-Za'tar'.

In the poem 'In Going to the World: A stranger to the world', Darwish controversially defends the 1972 Munich Olympic operation when Palestinian Black September members took nine Israeli athletes hostage.

In return for freeing the hostages, the gunmen demanded the release of 200 Palestinian fedayeen held in Israeli prisons.

Israeli PM Golda Meir refused to negotiate. German authorities promised to provide transport for the group and their hostages to get them to Cairo, where, they said, negotiations would continue. But the Germans had no intention of keeping their word.

The gunmen and hostages left the Olympic village in helicopters and travelled to Fuerstenfeldbrueck airfield. When they arrived at the airfield, the leaders of the Black September group went to check the awaiting plane. As they left their helicopter, they were cut down by sniper fire. The rest of the gunmen engaged in a fire fight with the police. One helicopter was blown up and another caught fire. All nine athlete hostages were killed, as were five of the eight gunmen.

The 'rescue' was a disaster for the Germans. The deaths of the nine athletes because of a bungled security operation was a national humiliation. The operation did not lead to the release of the fidayeen. The events though, did lead to increased anti-Arab racism in Germany and hundreds of Arab residents were summarily expelled from West Germany. The hostage taking led to international condemnation of the guerrillas and bolstered support for Israel. Three days later the Israelis launched a massive reprisal attack on Palestinian communities in Syria and Lebanon, killing close to 500 civilians (Hirst, 2003: p443).

However, from a Palestinian perspective, the operation was not necessarily a failure. For some within the PLO, the Munich episode did at least bring the world's attention to the Palestinian crisis. Salah Khalifeh, leader of Black September, claimed:

> World opinion was forced to take note of the Palestinian drama, and the Palestinian people imposed their presence on an international gathering that had sought to exclude them.

The testament of the five dead fighters was published by the Palestine News Agency in Syria. They apologised to the world's sportsmen and women, but went on:

We want them [ie sportspeople] to know of the existence of a people whose country has been occupied for 24 years, and their honour trampled underfoot... There is no harm if the youth of the world understand their tragedy for a few hours... So let the Games stop for a few hours.

To the Palestinian people the gunmen went on:

[do not] abandon your guns... The world only respects the strong. We shall not be strong through words alone, but only by acting on them... We want Arab youth to know how to die for their people and their country. (Hirst, 2003: p442)

In the aftermath, Darwish wrote a poem defending what many considered to be indefensible. 'In Going to the World: A stranger to the world' he wrote:

The one who has turned me into a refugee has made a bomb of me.
I know that I will die.
I know that I'm venturing into a lost battle today because it is a battle for the future.
I know that Palestine on the map is far away from me.

I know that you have forgotten its name and that you use a new term for it.
I know all that.
That is why I carry it to your streets, your homes and your bedrooms.
Palestine is not a land, gentlemen of the jury.
Palestine has become bodies that move, that move to the streets of the world,
Singing the song of death because the new Christ has given up his cross...
and gone out of Palestine.
                    (in Walker & Gowers, 2003: pp90/91)

The poem essentially alludes to the events of Munich as 'reaping the bitter fruits' of colonial settlement and oppression.

Too often the global media and various political commentators decry the violence of the oppressed whilst ignoring the violence of the oppressor. Today, think of the repeated attacks undertaken by the Israelis on Gaza and how little negative coverage this brings from the mainstream media. Or the Israeli campaign in 2019 to demolish Palestinian homes in East Jerusalem, or those deemed too close to the 'Separation Wall' in the village of Sur Baher, again barely worthy of mention in the media (Langendorf, 2019). Or how the killing of Palestinian children, like Ali Ayman Saleh Nasser, a fifteen-year-old boy from the village of Al-Mughayyir shot by Israeli soldiers in December 2020, is virtually ignored by the world's press (DCI(P), 2020).

Darwish's poem suggests that, by ignoring Palestine's just cause, by turning away from the horrors inflicted on the Palestinian people, by giving the country a new name, the international community has created the conditions in which the dispossessed respond with violence. In desperate circumstances, desperate people do desperate things.

In 'Ahmad al-Za'tar', Darwish writes about the victims of the massacre at Tal al-Zaatar refugee camp in east Beirut. This atrocity was carried out in 1976 at the start of the long Lebanese civil war. The attack was carried out by Christian Phalangist militia, with the tacit support of the Syrian regime.

During the Lebanese civil war, the PLO sided with the leftist forces of Kamal Jumblatt's Lebanese National Movement. This brought the PLO into conflict with Maronite Lebanese forces and with Syria, which was becoming increasingly involved in the country.

In June 1976, Maronite militias encircled the Palestinian camps of Jisr al-Basha and Tal al-Zaatar and the Shia Muslim settlement of Nabaa in east Beirut. On 22 June, the militias launched a ferocious attack and the Syrian army cut supply lines to the camps. Jisr al-Basra fell after six days. On 6 August, Nabaa was taken. Finally, after 52 days of continuous bombardment, the starving population of Tal al-Zataar surrendered under an agreement brokered by the Arab League.

As the unarmed camp inhabitants began to move out, the

Maronite gunmen opened fire, shooting indiscriminately at Palestinian men, women and children. An estimated 3,000 were killed and as many more were seriously injured (Walker & Gowers, 2003: pp152). The camp of Tal al-Zataar became another in the long list of atrocities inflicted upon Palestinian refugees.

Darwish addresses the massacre in 'Ahmed al-Za'tar'. The poem appeared in a collection published in 1977 called *Weddings*.

It seems strange in our eyes to have a poem about death and martyrdom in a collection about weddings. However, this is because in Palestinian communities (both Christian and Muslim), funeral processions for both martyrs and victims of Israeli atrocities have become defiant 'wedding processions'.

The martyr is treated like a groom going to his wedding. Often the *Dabke* is danced, songs are sung and speeches are made. The funeral becomes a political event. Hamzah suggests:

> The inversion of the meaning of the concept of wedding and its association with martyrdom and exile point to the sanctity of martyrdom for the sake of the homeland. (Hamzah, 2014: p172)

Darwish captures this in his poem 'Praise for a Thing That Did Not Arrive' in the collection *Trial No 7*:

> This is the wedding that never ends
> in a battlefield that has no end
> on a night that never ends.
> This is the Palestinian wedding
> where lover never reaches beloved
> except as a martyr or refugee.

The poem looks at the sacrifice of the martyr, whose blood permeates both time and space. Facing day to day struggles for survival often means, we lose our ability to dream of better futures. But the martyr resisted and died for an ideal. As a result, they live in a different world, one of infinite possibilities:

> They alone can see
> And the blood sense has ripened within them,

Leading them through twenty lost years.
Today she takes her future shape,
Their beloved,
Taking them back into her lifeblood.

Because they have shed their blood, they can move beyond the history of defeats (the '20 lost years'). They can 'return', wedded to their beloved Palestine.

'Ahmed al-Za'tar' is a long, epic poem about a martyr. It tells the story of Ahmed's birth and growth in the refugee camps and, utilising biblical imagery, it traces his spiritual union with the land and with Palestine and his fight to return to Haifa. It is a eulogy to a Palestinian hero and, in this sense, is identifiable as an example of Harlow's literature of resistance:

I am the land and here it has come
And dressed itself to me.
I am the endless return to the homeland
And I found myself filled with myself.

But unlike in other poems, Darwish does not name Ahmed's murderers. In earlier poems, Darwish has named and identified the aggressor and murderer of Palestinian people. But here there is no explicit denunciation, instead he obliquely notes the betrayal of Arab brothers:

From the Atlantic Ocean to the Arabian Gulf
They were counting spears

The demands of Arab unity and the relationships between the PLO and a variety of Arab regimes meant Darwish was reluctant to explore in detail how Palestinians were being treated in Lebanon or by right-wing forces in the Lebanese civil war or, indeed, by the Syrian state. But there is a hint that someday revenge will come upon those who have betrayed Palestine:

I am Ahmed the Arab—let the siege come
My body is the walls—let the siege come.
I am the edge of fire—let the siege come.
And I now besiege you with my beseigement,
I now besiege you

Mahmoud Darwish (1970-2008)

And my chest is the door to all the world's people—Let the siege come.

The betrayal at Tal al-Zataar would soon be dwarfed by an even greater tragedy inflicted upon the Palestinians in Lebanon.

At a political level, the Egyptian peace agreement with Israel, brokered by the US at Camp David in September 1978, represented a significant defeat for the pan-Arabist strategy of uniting 'Arab brothers' against the common imperialist-Zionist entity in its midst.

The Camp David agreement was denounced across the Arab world and Arab governments initially responded by activating economic sanctions against Egypt. But eventually other Arab states (Lebanon, Syria and Jordan) made their peace with Israel. The Camp David Accord was the wedge that was driven into the last vestiges of Arab unity (Hirst, 2003).

But rather than bring peace, the Camp David Accords encouraged the Israelis to be more assertive in their expansionist drive. In July 1980, the Israeli Parliament, the Knesset, passed a fundamental law declaring Jerusalem to be Israel's capital. In December 1980, the Golan Heights were effectively annexed. (Of course the 'international community' would not accept these moves until US President Trump recognised Jerusalem as the capital of Israel in 2017, and Israeli annexation of the Golan in 2019 (Borger, 2017, 2019).) In the aftermath of Camp David, there was also significant expansion of Settlement activity on the West Bank.

But the Camp David Accords also gave the Israelis the confidence to target PLO fighters more aggressively. As Hourani notes:

> Having secured its southern frontier by the peace treaty with Egypt, [Israel] now tried to impose its own solution of the problem of the Palestinians. This involved an attempt to destroy both the military and the political power of the PLO in Lebanon. (Hourani, 2002: p431)

At the start of 1978, the Israelis launched Operation Litani, which saw them occupy most of the area south of the Litani river in southern Lebanon. They withdrew, under considerable international pressure, later in the year, being replaced by the UN Interim Force in Lebanon (UNIFIL). Before they withdrew, the Israelis handed most of their positions over to their proxy, the South Lebanon Army.

Skirmishes between Palestinians, Israelis and the South Lebanon Army continued over the next period, with the Israelis looking for justification to launch a more significant invasion of Lebanon. The invasion eventually took place in June 1982, when Israel launched 'Operation Peace in the Galilee'.

At the start of the operation, Israel advanced rapidly, deep into Lebanon. The Israeli 'blitzkreig' saw them encircle Palestinian camps in southern Lebanon, destroy Syrian positions in the Beka'a Valley and cut the Beirut-Damascus road. Within three days they had encircled Beirut and were predicting the end of the PLO.

But things did not go to plan for the Israelis. Though out-numbered and out-gunned by the IDF, the Palestinian fighters fought heroically, defending their camps and West Beirut street by street, building by building. The Israelis responded by bombarding West Beirut relentlessly as they were dragged into a brutal and bloody war of attrition. The siege lasted 77 days and brought immense suffering and hardship to the Palestinians in the camps and the Lebanese citizens in West Beirut.

By the end of August, Arafat, in the face of significant internal opposition, agreed a deal, brokered by the US, for the PLO to leave the city. Approximately 11,500 fidayeen left Beirut and were scattered across eight Arab countries. Arafat and the PLO leadership, including Darwish, travelled to Tunis, via Damascus.

The PLO fighters left Beirut with a written guarantee from US President Ronald Reagan's Special Middle East Envoy Phillip Habib that Palestinian civilians in Beirut would be safe. Habib's guarantee was to prove worthless.

On 16 September, units of far-right Lebanese Phalangists, under the watchful and supportive eyes of the Israelis, entered the Palestinian refugee camps of Sabra and Shatila. Over the next 48 hours they committed unspeakable atrocities against Palestinian civilians. Hirst describes some of what went on.

> Phalagists entered...[the] camp at sunset. Some carried knives and axes as well as firearms. The carnage began immediately. It would continue without interruption for forty-eight hours. Night brought no respite: the Israelis lit up the camp with flares. Anything that moved in the narrow alleyways the Phalangists shot. They broke into houses and killed their occupants... Sometimes they tortured before they killed, gouging out eyes, skinning alive, disembowelling. Women and small girls were raped...before...they were finished off with axes. Babies were torn limb from limb and their heads smashed against walls. Entering Akka hospital the assailants assassinated the patients in their beds. They tied other victims to vehicles and dragged them through the streets alive. They cut off hands to get at rings and bracelets... Bulldozers were brought in to bury their victims. (Hirst, 2003: p558)

Darwish addresses the siege of Beirut in one of his great works 'A Memory for Forgetfulness' (1986). This is one of three prose-poems (the other two being 'Journal of Ordinary Grief' (1974) and 'In the Presence of Absence' (2006)) where Darwish revisits and reflects on aspects of his past.Covering events of a single day (6 August, Hiroshima Day), 'A Memory for Forgetfulness' is a prose-poem that is part history, part memory and part political essay. It is a multi-vocal text that combines poetry, prose, dialogue, history, myth, narrative fiction and dream sequences. Each comes together to provide a picture that captures the mindset of life under siege. It includes snippets of some of his earlier poems. Towards the end of the text, he references his poem 'Identity Card', discussed in the previous chapter. He wonders if the military officer he had to report to all those years before had a son who was flying a jet over Beirut and writes: "Put this in your record: I exist!... Put this in your record: I'm Arab!" (Darwish, 2013: p174).

On 6 August 1982, the Israelis bombarded Beirut from land, sea and air. It was one of the heaviest bombardments of the city during the siege. *The Sunday Times* (8 August, 1982) described it as a 'blitz against West Beirut'.

Muhawi argues that, for Darwish:

> During the shelling the extent of the entire Arab homeland shrinks—to Lebanon, to the city of Beirut, to a quarter in that city, to a street, to a building which has just been hit, to a room within that building (say, the author's study), and finally by implication to the printed page where these events are taking place in the reader's imagination. (Muhawi, 2013: p xxxii)

111

In many ways, 'A Memory for Forgetfulness' is a type of history from below, with a focus on the lived experiences, the lives and actions of ordinary Palestinian refugees. The text considers the 'ordinary' aspects of life under siege; the difficulties individuals have living, and comprehending their situation, in the face of a bombardment from "the harmonious triad of death: jets, navy and artillery" (Darwish, 2013: p176), against which "Human will can't do anything...they [the shells and bombs] are a fate that can't be turned back" (Darwish, 2013: p32).

This was a day where the threat of imminent death collapsed time to the moment between exploding shells, the time "between breathing in and breathing out" (Darwish, 2013: p6). In such conditions, going to the toilet becomes a source of anxiety (p4) and making a cup of coffee is an almost heroic act (p18), and refusing to leave and the daily necessity of gathering food and water are emphasised as signs of Palestinian steadfastness (p27).

The reality of life forces one to consider the possibility of imminent death:

> I don't want to die under the rubble. I'll pretend I'm going down to the street to look for a newspaper... I want to die in the open street... He who dies here does not die by chance. Rather he who lives, lives by chance. (p27)

But Darwish also uses the text to explore Palestinian history and the political strategies of those leading the 'Palestinian revolution'. For example, the ex-political prisoner Samir appears to debate what has gone wrong with 'the organisation' and he questions why the revolution needs to be tempered to balance the Palestinian relationship with other Arab nations ('Are we the Arab League? Samir asks' (p33)).

In the text we encounter the main protagonists of the war: the heroic fidayeen, with little water, food and ammunition, are described as they halt the Israeli advance. Begin, Sharon and Arafat are all present and form part of the discussion. The betrayal of Palestine by Arab leaders is explicit. The text debates the future of Palestine and the possibilities of return and, through use of myth, he emphasises the long connection between Palestinians and the land of Palestine, something that would become more central to his creative work in the aftermath of the defeat in Lebanon.

The PLO exodus from Beirut brought an end to direct armed operations against Israel. Although some fidayeen were able to smuggle their way back into Lebanon, they became involved in defending the refugee camps from Israeli-backed Maronite forces and the Syrian-backed Amal organization. It became known as the 'war of the camps' and ran between April 1985 and April 1987 as a sub-plot within the long Lebanese civil war.

By the mid-1980s, many commentators were suggesting the PLO was finished. The Arab regimes started to distance themselves from the organisation and were refusing to contribute financially to its funds. In November 1987, the Arab League summit made Palestine a minor issue on their meeting agenda, a previously unthinkable state of affairs (Marshall, 1989: p139).

From the mid-1980s, Darwish's poetry becomes more complex, less accessible, less shaped by the principles of adab al-iltizam and more focused on the historic links between Palestinians and their lands. He set out to challenge the claim that Palestine was a 'land without people' before Israeli colonisation, as former Israeli Prime Minister Golda Meir claimed. As Said and Barsamian note:

Because so much of [the Palestinians'] history has been occluded...they are invisible people. The strength and power of the Israeli narrative is such that it depends almost entirely on a kind of heroic vision of pioneers who come to a desert and in the end deal not with native people in the sense that these are people who have a settled existence and lived in towns and cities and have their own society, but rather with nomads who could be driven away. (Said & Barsamian, 2003: 20–21)

And Nomads, by virtue of their life, have no history that ties them to a particular place. Darwish sets out to establish the Palestinian presence and their historic connection to the land. He sees his role as a poet who is taking part in what he calls a "struggle between two memories" (Padel, 2009: p15).

By 1985 Darwish had relocated to Paris. The geographical and political distance from the Middle East that Paris offered him allowed what he called his "true poetic birth". Whilst in Paris he completed a series of poems, 'It's a Song' (1985), 'Fewer Roses' (1986), 'Eleven Planets' (1992), 'I See What I Want' (1993) and 'The Stranger's Bed' (1999).

In these works, he writes about Palestine for a universal audience. He uses myth to rewrite aspects of Palestinian history to combat the claims of Zionist historiography regarding Israel's ownership of ancient Palestine. Darwish set about challenging Zionist ideological claims that attempted to root European Jewry in historic Palestine:

Myth...became an area of contention and a potential means to retool the deep ideological structures of all those living in or belonging to Palestine. (Mattawa, 2014: p111)

Darwish notes that Zionist ideology was built on a series of biblical myths. Historical facts had not, in themselves, managed to undermine the hold of the myth. So, Darwish concluded, the poet should start to develop alternative mythical histories of Palestinian attachment to the land using stories from the Quran and the Bible.

One example is the poem 'A Canaanite Stone by the Dead Sea'. In 1947 the Dead Sea scrolls were discovered by young Bedouin shepherds in the Qumran caves on what is today the West Bank.

Darwish's 'Canaanite Stone' is found near the scrolls and is treated as a relic with as much authenticity as the scrolls themselves. And just like the scrolls, the stone tells of a range of beliefs, practices, languages and cultures that made up the Holy Land of original Palestine.

The move into longer, more mythical pieces does not mean Darwish turned away from the contemporary or controversial. Perhaps his most contentious poem of the late 1980s was "Those who pass between fleeting words" (1988) about the First Intifada.

Historically, the Palestinian national movement had developed within the Palestinian diaspora. Its roots and its energy were in the refugee camps across the Middle East. But December 1987 witnessed a wave of protests amongst Palestinians in Gaza, the West Bank and within Palestine48.

The First Intifada was a mass social movement. It involved men and women, old and young, in demonstrations, strikes and protests that reinvigorated the Palestinian liberation movement. Activists established youth and cultural centres, welfare and health centres, women's networks and alternative education programmes. In the process, they won millions worldwide to the cause of Palestinian freedom and reinvigorated the PLO, establishing a strong internal leadership.

The Israeli leadership were stunned and responded brutally. *The Jerusalem Post* (23 January 1988) noted:

> The streets, both in Gaza and the West Bank and in East Jerusalem, are...in effective control of the youth. It's a situation of our 20-year-olds battling their 20-year-olds— ours using armour, helicopters and guns; theirs clubs, rocks and primitive Molotov cocktails.

During the Intifada, Darwish wrote 'Those Who Pass Between Fleeting Words' (1988). The poem was translated into Hebrew and caused some controversy. The poem includes the lines:

Live where you like, but do not live among us
It is time for you to be gone
...
So leave our land
Our shore, our sea
Our wheat, our salt, our wound.

Darwish had a reputation amongst sections of the liberal intelligentsia within Israel of being a 'dove' and someone they could 'work with'. But in the context of a popular uprising, many on the Israeli liberal left moved to support the Israeli crack down on Palestinian youth. The poem incensed them and many denounced it, suggesting that it advocated the removal of all Israelis from Palestine (Eid, 2016).

Hedda Boshes, a columnist for *Haaretz*, suggested the poem was a "slap in the face" of liberal Israelis that "destroyed with one blow [their] entire thesis" that there are moderate Palestinians with whom Israel can deal (Moffett, 1988). Whilst Amos Keinan, Israeli author, sculptor, journalist, and founder of the Council for Israeli-Palestinian Peace, wrote:

Those sleeping Israelis who had begun to wake up [because of the uprising] and ask if it wasn't time to speak to you—they may now decide that there is nothing to speak to you about other than via the barrel of a rifle. (Moffett, 1988)

However, Darwish was clear. The poem was about the Israelis' brutal response to the Intifada. In the first ten days of the Uprising, 27 Palestinians were killed and more than 250 were injured. Israeli Defence Minister Yitzak Rabin announced an 'iron fist' policy would operate in Gaza and the West Bank, saying "we will make it clear who is running the territories" (in Marshall, 1989: p14). This context shines light on the poem. The second verse, for example, reads:

O those who pass between fleeting words
From you the sword—from us the blood
From you steel and fire—from us our flesh
From you yet another tank—from us stones

From you tear gas—from us rain
Above us, as above you, are sky and air
So take your share of our blood—and be gone
Go to a dancing party—and be gone
As for us, we have to water the martyrs' flowers
As for us, we have to live as we see fit.

The poem is a rage against the Israeli machine and a defence of the young stone throwers. As the controversy raged, Darwish clarified that the demand 'to leave' was for the Israelis to leave Gaza and the West Bank. The furore perhaps revealed more about the attachment of the Israeli intelligentsia to the Zionist project than to their commitment to Palestinian rights and equality.

The First Intifada ran from December 1987 to September 1993. It developed a new internal leadership within the PLO and it forced the Israelis to negotiate with Arafat. The Intifada is normally dated as ending with the signing of the Oslo Accords, or the Declaration of Principles, in Washington on 13 September, 1993. The Declaration included Palestinian and Israeli 'mutual recognition' and allowed for governing functions to be handed over to a Palestinian Authority covering the West Bank and Gaza. The Declaration allowed for progressively more functions to be handed over to the PA during an initial five-year period, during which time a full peace treaty would be signed and the 'two-state solution' formalised.

Though an advocate for a two-state solution, Darwish could not accept the Oslo Accords. He felt they were too general, did not tie the Israelis down to a specific road map to peace and could easily be undermined by the Israeli state. In these criticisms he was perceptive and would prove to be correct. In protest, in 1993, he resigned from all official affiliations with both the PLO and the Palestinian Authority. In 1995, however, he was persuaded to move to Ramallah, where he would see out the rest of his days. He devoted himself to writing and editing the cultural journal *Al-Karmal* and he continued to write about Palestinian history and myth and to emphasise the importance of Palestinian culture.

In the 1990s, Darwish's poetry moved away from direct themes of resistance. His 1998 collection *A Bed for the Strangers* was a book of love poems. And to critics who wondered why he had moved away from politics, he remarked: "If I write love poems, I resist the conditions that don't allow me to write love poems" (quoted in Padel, 2009: p18). He also wrote longer mythical and historical poems which reference to the Crusades, Mongol invasion and discussions between Palestinians and other displaced peoples, such as First Nation North Americans.

Despite the promises embedded in the Oslo Accords, the Israelis continued to block any progress towards the fulfilment of a Palestinian state. Amidst growing tensions, on 28 September, 2000, Ariel Sharon led an invasion of the Al Aqsa Mosque compound in Jerusalem/Al Quds with an estimated 1,000 police officers. He loudly declared: "The Temple Mount is in our hands" (American Muslims for Palestine, 2012). The invasion of the compound, the third holiest site in Islam, produced a furious response from Palestinians who came out to defend the Mosque. These events led directly to the Second (Al Aqsa) Intifada that was fought out between 2000 and 2005.

In contrast to the First Intifada, the Second Intifada was much more militarized. In the first few days of the Second Intifada, Israeli troops fired over 1,300,000 bullets (Pedatzur, 2004). In response, Palestinians picked up sticks, stones and guns and some strapped themselves with explosives and turned themselves into human bombs. During the uprising, almost 5,000 Palestinians were killed, including just under 1,000 children (Middle East Monitor, 2019).

Although the Palestinian community demonstrated and protested against the Israeli violence, the militarized nature of the uprising necessarily involved fewer people and those that were directly involved tended to be younger and male.

During the Second Intifada, Darwish stayed in Ramallah. In the immediacy of the struggle, he wrote two poems that were reminiscent of his early resistance poetry. 'Mohammed' and 'A State of Siege' were published in the Arab press during 2001/02.

'Mohammed' is a relatively short poem written about eleven-year-old Muhammed al-Durra, murdered by Israeli soldiers on 30 September, 2000. Muhammed's death was shown on television screens across the globe. The horror and brutality of the killing shocked millions.

On the day he was murdered, a group of young Palestinians approached the illegal Israeli settlement of Netzarim in the middle of the Gaza Strip. They threw stones at the Israeli occupation soldiers who set up a military checkpoint at the Settlement's eastern gate. The soldiers responded by firing live ammunition.

Mohammed's father, Jamal, tried to shield his son from the firing and both cowered behind a concrete roadblock. The cameras picked up the desperate screams of Jamal, begging the Israelis to stop firing at his son. His cries were ignored and Muhammed was hit several times. He died on his father's lap, and his dying breaths were screened around the world.

Whilst the killing of Mohammed Al-Durra was beamed across the globe, how could the poet Darwish respond? What kind of language could possibly match the horror and shock of the televised execution? Darwish suggests the task was not to produce a poem that 'screamed' at the horror (because the scream could get lost in the noise of continuing violence). Instead, he felt he needed to produce a reflective, mournful poem for the dead; an elegy. The tone is set in the opening stanza:

Mohammed,
nestles in the bosom of his father, a bird afraid
of the infernal sky: father protect me
from the upward flight! My wing is
slight for the wind...and the light is black

The elegy is for Mohammed, but it speaks to the pointlessness, the brutality and the inhumanity of the killing of Palestinian children. There is quiet rage when Darwish questions the unfathomable inhumanity of the murderous act:

Mohammed,
a destitute angel, within a stone's throw of

the gun of his cold-blooded hunter. For
an hour the camera traces the movements of the boy
who is merging with his shadow:
his face, clear, like dawn
his heart, clear, like an apple
his ten fingers, clear, like candles
the dew clear on his trousers...
His hunter could have reflected
twice, and say: I will spare him till when he spells
his Palestine without mistakes...
I will spare him now subject to my conscience
and kill him the day he rebels!

The poem beautifully articulates the collective grief of a beleaguered people who have been subjected to so many horrors inflicted upon them by an occupying power.

'State of Siege' was originally published in January 2002 (Darwish, 2010b). It is a long poem made up of 115 stanzas, within which Darwish describes daily life in Ramallah during the siege in the Second Intifada. In some respects, this reminds us of 'A Memory for Forgetfulness' and the way that he combines and locates the ordinary acts of daily living within much greater, uncontrollable historical events.

He begins by setting the scene. Ramallah is a beautiful city on the crest of the Judean Hills (Jibal al-Khalil) with stunning views down the valley. But Ramallah is not a place at peace:

Here, where the hills slope before the sunset and the chasm
of time
near gardens whose shades have been cast aside
we do what prisoners do
we do what the jobless do
we sow hope

In a land where the dawn sears
we have become more doltish
and we stare at the moments of victory
there is no starry night in our nights of explosions

our enemies stay up late, they switch on the lights
in the intense darkness of this tunnel.

(Darwish, 2010: p2)

But Ramallah: "Under siege,/life is measured between
the memory of its beginning/ and the oblivion of its end ..."
(Darwish, 2010: p17)

The poem offers a series of vignettes of daily life under siege.
But the work also offers a retrospective on his corpus and lets us
re-visit some of the characters and images from across his work.
It includes those who have been martyred and their 'wedding
ceremony', discussed through a mother who tells the author/
speaker that her son had just gotten 'married' (ie just been
martyred) and was now:

Above the sky, two angels
Consummating their marriage. (p214)

But now this event, powerfully evoked in his earlier poems as a
celebration of the heroic fighter, is tinged with a weariness at the
long lines of the martyred. So Darwish responds:

So I sang out my ululations
And danced and sang and danced until I fell down
With a stroke. And so dying I asked,
"O my beloved, when will this honeymoon end?" (p214)

Indeed, later in the poem, a martyr appears and challenges the
poet for turning him into a mythical, heroic figure. The martyr
cries: "Toss back into the dictionaries all the words/you gave to
me as gifts" (p245). Towards the end, the poem becomes almost
a plea for reconciliation as he offers to teach the 'uncivilised
soldier' about their shared humanity:

I'll teach you...
You have a mother
And I have a mother
And we have the same rain
And we have the same moon
And a short absence from each other's dining tables. (p238)

It is a cry for peace and an end to the never-ending suffering of the people of Palestine. In doing so, it contains sections which address antisemitism and the Holocaust, and a plea that ethnic cleansing wherever and whenever it takes place must be condemned. The poem abounds in attempts to humanise the 'enemy soldier' and it demands reconciliation which, at times, comes close to despair about the future. But nevertheless, though the future may be bleak, 'We nurse hope!' (p3)

Darwish died in Ramallah in 2008. He had been ill with heart problems for some time. His life and the struggle for Palestinian liberation had been deeply entangled and he remains today one of the great Palestinian cultural figures of the post-Nakba era. In his work, he turned "private anguish into a public testament, evoking a collective feeling that broke down the barriers between I and We and between the poet and his audience" (Mattawa, 2014: p11). After his death, a posthumous volume of poetry was published called *A River Dies of Thirst*. The collection includes several short poems and thoughts. It includes the poem 'A Common Enemy', which is a cry for peace and another poem that emphasises our common humanity and rails against the futility of war:

121

It is time for the war to have a siesta… Fighters on both sides say similar things in the presence of the ones they love. But the casualties on both sides don't realise until it's too late that they have a common enemy: death. (Darwish, 2009; p36)

Chapter 5

The personal and the political: Fadwa Tuqan

122

The Palestinian woman faces a double struggle: the struggle to assert her liberation as a woman and the struggle to assert her and everybody else's national liberation... [O]nce the inevitable national liberation is achieved...[o]ur feminist liberation will also prevail... I know our people and I know that their aspiration to freedom is comprehensive and sincere. And I know our women too, their seriousness, their endurance, their pride in themselves and their abiding confidence. Let there be no turning from the path of dignity and freedom in all spheres. (Tuqan, 1985: pp204/205)

SO FAR, WE HAVE LOOKED at two giants of the Palestinian resistance movement and two recognised cultural notables in Ghasssan Kanafani and Mahmoud Darwish. The next two chapters turn to look at the work of the most significant Palestinian woman poet and writer of personal-account literature, Fadwa Tuqan, and one of the great artists of the Palestinian refugee poor Naji al-Ali.

The artistic output of both was fundamentally shaped by their engagement in the national liberation struggle. However, both stood to some degree outside of the main Palestinian resistance organisations. The degree of separation and distance they had from the main resistance networks allowed them to be more reflective of the direction in which the Palestinian struggle and politics in the Arab world were moving. It allowed both to bring something quite distinctive to their artistic output.

The works of Tuqan and al-Ali contain criticism of the dominant politics of the national liberation movement and their leadership's strategies. At times this brought them into the conflict with the Palestinian leadership, especially the PLO, by raising important questions about class and gender. Such questions, of course, immediately pose issues that challenge monolithic conceptions about 'nation' and common or shared national interests.

Tuqan's work allows us to consider the role of women in the struggle for Palestinian liberation.

It is sometimes suggested that Kanafani and Darwish tended to feminize Palestine in their writings, portraying it as 'mother, wife, lover or sister'. Darwish's great poem 'Identity Card', which we have referred to several times, includes the verse:

> Write down I am Arab
> My identity number is 50,000
>
> …
>
> I have eight children and the ninth is due next summer…
> Are you angry?

This verse seems to indicate that the Palestinian people will not be wiped out and that they are still here, reproducing and growing, creating what Israeli politicians and commentators refer to as the 'demographic timebomb' (Alon & Benn, 2003). But there is little consideration of the women producing such large numbers of children and the difficulties of raising them in the camps across the Arab world. The voice of women is often silent.

Liu Ze Yu and Nahla Alhartani note that often in Palestinian literature:

> Women remain a symbolic extension of the earth or its compliment. The nostalgia for mother, the beloved and sister overlap with nostalgia for the occupied land. (Ze Yu & Alhartani, 2018: p4)

This is sometimes encapsulated in the notion of the Um al-Shaheed—the 'mother of the martyr'. But in the construction of this symbol of the liberation movement, the role of women as fighters for liberation is often downplayed. Rajaa Natour goes as far as to argue that Darwish:

Espoused a masculine Palestinian victim narrative...that automatically excludes poetic, cultural and political feminine narratives. The result is a political and historical narrative devoid of Palestinian women's presence, memories and voices. (Rajaa Natour, 2020)

This image of passive though steadfast women in some Palestinian literature is matched by a lazier stereotype generated in the Western media and by some liberal commentators that depicts

Arab women as particularly oppressed and downtrodden. In the early twenty-first century, both Barbara Bush and Cherie Blair spoke out in defence of 'oppressed Arab women' as part of the attempt to justify the wars in Afghanistan, Iraq and elsewhere in the region (German & Murray, 2005).

Fadwa Tuqan's life and work is underpinned by the belief that the issue of women's emancipation in the Middle East is best left to the women of the region themselves, rather than any reliance on 'Western intervention'. Her work rages against conservative, gendered roles that reinforce women's oppression. She speaks out about the problems of coercion in personal and private relations, about the restrictions placed on women by traditional familial structures and against the alienation of women within society. In this way she emphasises the positive aspect of stressing the 'personal is political'; that women's oppression and demands for women's rights are not marginal, intra-familial or private concerns, rather they are public, political matters that concern us all.

Tuqan was born into a relatively affluent family in Nablus in the northern sector of the West Bank. Her family's wealth came from landownership and from olive-oil soap factories, bath houses, flour mills and shops. She was born in 1917, just as the Balfour Declaration was written, and grew up in Mandate Palestine under British Occupation. In her words:

> I arrived at a time when one world was in its death throes and another was about to be born; the Ottoman Empire was breathing its last; and Allied armies were continuing

to open the way for a new western colonization—1917.
(Tuqan, 1985: p15)

In her early works, she wrote romantic poems with traditional rhymes, many of them elegant elegies. But later, she moved to writing free verse and became noted for voicing her emotions and feelings, as well as demanding resistance to Israeli occupation. After 1967, she became a recognized national poet, writing resistance poetry. Her status meant that the 1985 publication of the first part of her autobiography became a significant event.

Her work demands and asserts the importance of individual human freedom, of free choice in love and matters of the heart, of freedom of action and of thought. She writes:

> Our Eastern Arab society suppresses the sentiment of love, just as it continually oppresses women. The magic hand of this beautiful human emotion touched even the hearts of prophets... In Arab society, this beautiful human emotion is a casualty of the split nature of our society and still carries connotations of disgrace and shame... To me it [love] is the affirmation of my crushed humanity and its very salvation.
> (Tuqan, 1985: pp114/115)

In her early poems, where the topics were focused on love and human emotions, she adopted a penname: Dananir. Using her own name would have potentially exposed her to the disapproval of her family's social circle. But the choice of name is also significant. Dananir was the name of a slave girl in Arabic literature of the Middle Ages who was taught to read and write so she could perform for men.

In *I Will Not Sell My Love*, Tuqan writes:

> I am a woman and so forgive me that my heart exalts to
> Your whisper that is music singing forth, your eyes from the depths
> And you are all beauty
> You sing to me from my homeland and
> Then the shadows of love appear in your eyes.
> (in Tzoreff, 2000: p69)

Similarly, in 'A Moment', she reflects on an intimate liaison:

> Love, let's be quiet, don't say
> 'there was, there will be...'
> ...
> It's this moment that counts
> Only now, nothing before or after,
> ...
> Maybe your dreams and mine
> are different
> But this moment's
> Unique, radiantly open in our hands
> Plucked and fruitless
> A flower of temporary magnificence
> So let's treasure it before it wilts.
>
> (Tuqan, 1985: p222)

In these poems, Tuqan is asserting her agency and her right to express emotions and feelings of love, intimacy and sexual attraction in a society that denies these to women. As Jayyusi argues:

> Tuqan showed a superb capacity to express elation at the liberation of body and soul...whereby love, desire, spiritual buoyancy, and physical freedom are merged together.
>
> (Jayyusi, 1992: p20)

Crucially for Tuqan, she locates and sees the struggle for individual liberation as a necessary part of a struggle for collective freedom. She writes in her autobiography:

> When the roof fell in on Palestine in 1948, the veil fell off the face of the Nablus woman... With the fall of Palestine in 1948, the traditional structure of Arab society was shaken, politically, socially and culturally. The reactionary regimes in Egypt and Syria fell, the popular movements grew stronger in Egypt and Iraq. The concepts of socialism and Marxism began to penetrate the minds of the Arab people, directing them towards the fight against imperialism, on the one hand and, on the other, against societies traditional concepts.
>
> (Tuqan, 1985: p113; p117)

Her early life is described in her first of two autobiographical works, *A Mountainous Journey* (1985). The second, *A More Difficult Journey*, published in 1993, is yet to be published in English. According to Hamden et al, *A Mountainous Journey* is "one of the most important autobiographies in modern Arabic literature;...[it's] considered as a rebellion against her patriarchal society" (Hamden et al, 2020: p158)

Salma Khadra Jayyusi describes the work as a prime example of Palestinian personal account literature. She goes on to stress the importance of this genre of writing:

> By writing their own personal accounts, Palestinians assert not only their own identity as eyewitness to Palestinian life and experience, but their identity of their own country: an Arab Palestine with roots that go deep into the past, not simply as religious history of major significance to both Muslim and Christian Arabs in Palestine, but as an actual, cumulative life modified and shaped by the very fauna and flora of the land, its ecology, its customs and mores... These writings embody the conventions, sayings, concepts, humour, and creative illuminations of many generations of Palestinians. (Jayyusi, 1990: pvii)

The work combines, firstly, a 'coming of age' motif of a young woman growing up in a society in transition and, secondly, a description of growing collective national consciousness amongst Palestinians against the background of British colonial occupation, the Nakba and the Naksa. As Tzoreff argues, the work is:

> A record of a passing era in which her perceptions and insights are used to stir and penetrate the collective memory of her subjugated people in order to urge them to action. (Tzoreff, 2000: p77)

It traces the journey of the witness-narrator in her quest for freedom and independence as she struggles to forge her identity as a poet and national spokesperson. As it does so, it addresses conflicts with her family and her community within a decaying 'traditional' society that oppresses and silences women. It also confronts the turbulent impact of foreign occupation and the establishment of a colonial-settler state on the people of Palestine.

There are three key points that come out of her autobiography.

First, the work offers a discussion regarding her family's longstanding links with Palestine and the Nablus region. The 'Tuqan hills', for example, are mentioned as a place where branches of her family had lived for centuries. It discusses her family tree, which includes great generals in Ottoman armed forces. It describes the architecture of her Nablus home, "one of the most ancient of the old Nablus homes" (Tuqan, 1985: p36). Here, the work emphasises the long-standing Arab presence in Palestine and her family's roots in the immediate vicinity of Nablus.

Second, and the most important theme in the autobiography, Tuqan explicitly addresses the restrictions that women face in male-dominated Palestinian society. In an interview published in *Haaretz* in 1993, she states:

> I felt in my heart that Arab society was ready to accept
> my frank thoughts... I knew I had to express my defiance
> openly... I set for myself the supreme goal of describing the
> story of my life with complete honesty... I have always stood
> with the women of our society and against her oppression.
> I demand freedom for the women, and the right to a full
> human life. (in Algazi, 1993)

Her autobiography includes sharp comment on the position of women in society.

Nablus was a socially conservative city and Fadwa was brought up in a strict household. In her early years, the women of the household were expected to be veiled when leaving the home. She was not allowed out unaccompanied and was restricted from establishing friendship networks. From an early age, she was expected to undertake household chores and service the needs of her brothers and father. In almost every aspect of life, women and girls were expected to adhere to strictly regulated roles. She was brought up living in a community that treated women as objects, whose needs, interests and voices were ignored. As she notes:

> The iron mould the family cast us in and would not allow us to break, the time-worn rules difficult to overturn, the mindless traditions imprisoning the girl in a life of trivialities... I yearned continually to escape from my time and place. The time was an age of subjection, repression and dissolution into nothingness; the place was the prison of the house. (Tuqan, 1985: p12)

Later she writes:

> In [our] house, within its high walls that shut off the harem society from the outside world...my oppressed childhood, girlhood and a great part of my youth were spent.
> The man dominated family life, as in all homes of our society. The woman had to forget the word 'no' existed...
> The right to express her feelings or views was prohibited...
> Personal independence as a concept foreign to a woman all her life...
> Women...live their empty lives in that house, that prison. (Tuqan, 1985: p36)

Her relationship with her mother was difficult, she describes it as problematic and bitter. Her mother attempted to abort her several times before she was born, dressed her in 'unbecoming' clothes, treated her roughly and never told stories about her childhood. Apparently, she was cut out of her mother's memory. Nevertheless, in a revealing passage in her autobiography, she draws a distinction between her mother's role within the family, as rearing children and promoting particular 'roles,' and her mother as a 'woman'. She describes a visit to the public baths when her mother, without clothes,

> appeared more beautiful and more attractive than ever. In my eyes she looked like a fairy-tale houri [ie one of the maidens promised to Martyrs in Paradise]. I also noticed [that]...her

naturally gregarious disposition, along with her wit and beauty, seems to have attracted others to her.
(Tuqan, 1985: p24)

Outside the confines of oppressive family structures, her mother came alive, became a positive figure and a person in her own right.

Thus, for Tuqan, the position of women in Arab society results from the interplay of two elements:

> *A Mountainous Journey* provide[s]...evidence to the notion that Tuqan, being a woman from an environment that is engulfed in suffering, finds the maltreatment of the members of the female gender to be an outcome of both male dominance and oppression by external forces [ie by Imperialism and settler colonialism]. (Ahmad, 2017: p36)

It is her commitment to both social and national independence that marks out her autobiography.

A third theme in *A Mountainous Journey* relates to questions of class. There are two elements here. On the one hand, there is description of class disdain for the poor. Here, she describes both the class arrogance emanating from family members, especially her aunt, and class hatred towards the Palestinian poor, which also points to class suspicion towards the refugees of 1947/48. It is worth noting that unlike Kanafani and Darwish (and al-Ali as we will see in chapter 6), Tuqan was not directly affected by displacement in 1948. In fact, coming from an affluent family in Nablus, their experience of the Nakba was one of dealing with a sudden arrival of refugees from Palestine48 and the strain that desparate, displaced people placed on local resources. Also there were the consequences of Jordanian occupation after the ceasefire placed Nablus under their control.

The second element of the class dynamic was the growing realization that the rich and powerful in the Arab world cannot be relied upon as allies in the struggle for freedom. Tuqan partly includes a record of the betrayal of the 'notables' of the national liberation cause.

Stressing women's oppression and class divisions in this way marked the autobiography out as a controversial literary intervention.

Brought up in a restrictive household, Fadwa's place of escape was school, where she enjoyed learning. But at the age of thirteen, a boy gave her some flowers in the street and her brother and father decided that she should no longer leave the home for educational purposes.

Luckily, if this is the right word in such a terrible situation, her other elder brother, Ibrahim, decided to take over her education and began to help and support her poetry writing. Ibrahim Tuqan was an established nationalist poet and he started to teach her the Arabic classics. As she later said: "Ibrahim turned my prison into my classroom."

Much of her early poetry is somewhat formal in style and quite introverted. An example is 'A Life', written in 1948, which reflects on her isolation and loneliness.

My life is tears
And a fond heart
Longing, a book of poetry and a lute

My life, my totally sorrowful life
…
On the sad nights
When silence endlessly deepens,
The phantoms of my loved ones pass
Before me like wisps of dreams
Poking the fire alive beneath the ashes
And drenching my pillow with tears

When her brother Ibrahim died in 1941, her father asked her to compose nationalist poetry and take on her brother's mantle. She felt unable to do so. Her life experiences and the confinement imposed on her by her family, she argued, made the production of political or nationalist poetry difficult:

The reality of life in that bottled-up harem was humiliating submission… In that environment, in the midst of those circumstances, it was difficult for me to develop a spirit of open rebelliousness...while I was in this state of alienation and psychological siege, Father often came and asked me to write political poetry... How and with what right or logic does Father ask me to compose political poetry, when I am shut up inside these walls? I don't sit with the men, I don't listen to their heated discussions, nor do I participate in the turmoil of life on the outside. (Tuqan, 1985: pp106/107)

Her father died in 1948, the same year as the Nakba. Together these two events marked the beginning of changes in Fadwa's life. She came out of the home and started to travel more. She began to become more aware of political issues and to engage in social and political life more fully. She was enthused by the victory of Nasser in Egypt. Her brother Rahmi was a Communist and he used to debate with her, although the Communist Party's acceptance of partition pushed them to the margins of political life in the West Bank ("In those days, agreement to the partition resolution was considered treason to the country and its people" (Tuqan, 1985: p129)).

In this context, she describes herself being motivated by political events but does not identify herself as a political poet. Her poetry still focused on the personal, on issues of the heart, love, belonging and self-realisation. Of course, as noted earlier, by discussing these issues, she was asserting women's right to have such feelings and emotions, denied at the time by the restrictive mores of wealthy Palestinian society.

Poems addressing these themes appear in the collection *Alone with the Days* (1952) and *I Found It* (1958). But these collections, alongside *Give Us Love* (1960) and *Before the Closed Door* (1967), also trace the evolution of Palestinian political consciousness from shock, despair and victimhood to summud, resistance and renewed pride.

The poem 'I Found It', reflects her growing self-assurance and self-awareness. It is a poem about moving beyond the restrictive life she experienced within her Nablus home. She is in the process of self-discovery and establishing her independent existence as she breaks free from oppressive traditions.

I found it on a beautiful bright day
I found it after long loss
…
I went away, the signpost of the abys of yesterday
Today I was led to myself.

Family wealth gave Tuqan the ability to move away from family life in Nablus, and at various points she lived in Amman and Ramallah. Between 1962 and 1964 she spent time studying in England.

But it is after 1967 that there is a clear change in her poetic and political direction, when she started to engage in the free verse movement and became known for her distinctive chronicling of the suffering of the Palestinians. Song (2008) suggests there were three reasons for this explicit change.

First, and most obviously, there was the changing political situation after the defeat in the Six-Day War. This brought Nablus and the West Bank under direct Israeli rule. More generally, as part of this process there was a general questioning of pan-Arabism and the belief that progressive Arab regimes would liberate Palestine. In its place was a growing recognition that Palestinians would need to rely on their own energies and political strategies if they were to defeat the occupier. This argument, as noted earlier, grew more popular after the fedayeen victory at Karama (see chapter 3).

Second, Tuqan had, during the 1960s, been in dialogue with another Palestinian poet, journalist and politician Kamal Nasir. As part of their growing friendship, Nasir had argued with Tuqan that she should turn from a poetry concerned with the self to one that was primarily concerned with nation. He debated with her on the issue of poetic form and the purpose and role of poetry, presenting her with arguments about adab al-iltizam. Nasir was expelled from the West Bank by Israel after the Naksa. After he was arrested, Tuqan wrote 'To the Imprisoned Singer' and dedicated it to Kamal Nasir:

> Your singing soars to us
> Despite the narrowness of the sky.
> Imprisoned bird! Sing forth
> From behind the walls of suffering and night
> ...
> Your singing, bird, returned me
> to the past
> when your feet and wings were free,
> when the jasmine bower
> embraced us, and you sang
> the poetry of hope and pride and strength
> ...
> Sing, bird, sing, the road of hope
> Stretches its light forward
> Though now we are surrounded by night.
> (Tuqan, 1985: p210)

The Naksa did, however, open the West Bank and allowed Palestinians living there and in Gaza to travel inside Palestine48. Tuqan took up the opportunity and travelled to meet Palestinian poets 'in the interior'. She met Darwish, Samih al-Qasim and Salma al-Khadra al Jayyusi. After the meeting she wrote the poem 'I Shall Not Weep' and dedicated it to "the poets of the resistance, on our meeting in Haifa".

Meeting with, arguing with and reading the poetry of Nasir and the young poets of the interior had a significant impact on her, drawing her towards a more engaged poetry.

Third, Tuqan was deeply affected by the execution, in 1967, of the Palestinian martyr Mazin Gut Abu Gazala. Song argues:

> On June 15 Gazala wrote in his diary that "I am sitting here trying to write my diary. What shall I write about?—How cowardly and insignificant it is to sit here and write on a day like this... Bullets give a shout of joy. Pens, be silent". Fadwa Tuqan decided to join the nationalistic struggle after reading this diary. (Song, 2008)

There was perhaps one further personal element linked with her move to a more engaged poetry: the tragic death of her older brother Namr. Namr died in a plane accident and Fadwa, who was in England at the time, travelled home to mourn the loss of a second brother. She arrived just before the Naksa, and this personal tragedy became enmeshed with the national tragedy. Both events filled Tuqan with a sense of despair. That sense of alienation and tragedy is captured in her collection *In Front of Closed Doors* (1967).

Before the 1967 Six-Day War, Tuqan's poetry focused mainly on Palestinian women's lack of educational and cultural opportunities. But after Israel's capture of the West Bank and Gaza, her poetry shifted to focus on the day-to-day hardships of life under occupation and her writings become overtly political and nationalist. These more overtly political aspects of her poetry are covered in the collections *The Night of the Horsemen* (1969), *Alone on the Summit of the World* (1973), *Political Poems* (1980) and *July and the Other Thing* (1989).

The Night and the Horsemen (1969) is a collection of poems about the Naksa and its aftermath. Three poems mark out her overt political turn. In the poem 'My Sad City', she describes the occupation of Nablus:

The day we saw death and betrayal
The tide ebbed
The windows of the sky closed
And the city held its breath
...
Hope turned to ashes
And gagging on disaster
My sad city choked.

The outcome of the Six-Day War is described in the poem 'The Deluge and the Tree'. Here Palestine, swept over by the Israeli forces, is depicted as a tree that is engulfed in flood waters:

When the hurricane swirled and spread its deluge
of dark evil
onto the good green land

'they' gloated. The western skies
reverberated with joyous accounts:
"The Tree has fallen!
The great trunk is smashed!
The hurricane leaves no life in the Tree!"

But though the tree has suffered, its roots remain strong and deeply attached to the land. Had the tree really fallen?

Never! Not with our red streams flowing forever,
not while the wine of our thorn limbs
fed the thirsty roots,
Arab roots alive
tunneling deep, deep, into the land!

The Palestinians are not easily vanquished. The blood of the martyrs, the red, flowing streams, nourishes the liberation struggle. The Palestinians have a long connection to the land and the struggle and one day, like the birds which come to nestle on the tree, the people will return:

When the Tree rises up, the branches
shall flourish green and fresh in the sun,
the laughter of the Tree shall leaf
beneath the sun
and birds shall return.
Undoubtedly, the birds shall return.
The birds shall return.   (Tuqan, 1985 p223)

The idea of rebirth and return are also captured in her poem 'Labour Pains'. In this piece, she uses the idea of pollen floating through the ruins of a destroyed city, trying to find a place to settle, to represent the Palestinian refugees. The colonisers suggest displacement is a sign of submission but for Tuqan, within the displacement lies the hope of the nation's rebirth.

The wind blows the pollen in the night
through ruins of fields and homes.
Earth shivers with love,
with the pain of giving birth,
but the conqueror wants us to believe

stories of submission and surrender.
O Arab Aurora!
Tell the usurper of our land
that childbirth is a force unknown to him,
the pain of a mother's body,
that the scarred land
inaugurates life
at the moment of dawn
when the rose of blood
blooms on the wound.

These poems are easily understood and established Tuqan as a leading poet of the liberation movement. Her great skill was the ability to capture the routine everyday events of the occupation and the experiences of ordinary Palestinians. Her poem 'Hamza', discussed in the Introduction, is about a steadfast, 'ordinary' Palestinian. In 'Waiting at the Allenby Bridge', she captures the humiliation of Palestinians at checkpoints, here specifically at the Allenby Bridge crossing between Jordan and the West Bank. She writes of "Miserable eyes, waiting, begging to pass". It is worth noting that today, there are somewhere in the region of 350 checkpoints across the West Bank. At many of them the 'miserable eyes' will be there, waiting and waiting 'begging to pass' and get on with their lives.

Tuqan also writes about women as central actors within the resistance. In 'From Hiba's Diary', she discusses a young schoolgirl resister who she describes as a gift from the mother to the homeland. Whilst in 'I Shall Not Weep', the poem dedicated to the poets of the resistance, her final verse emphasises her role, and women's role, within the national resistance movement, contrasting the "road of light and sun", the road of resistance leading to a liberated Palestine, with the "dark night" of colonisation:

Lamps of the dark night
Brothers in the wound...
On your road shall I walk
In the light of your eyes

I collect yesterday's tears
And wipe them away.
Like you, I plant my feet on the land,
My country,
And fix my eyes, like yours,
On the road of light and sun.

(Tuqan, 1985 p226)

These poems celebrate the role of women as active participants in the struggle for liberation. Here, it is worth recognising that there have been many women who have played central roles in resistance activities. For example, there were several leading women militants within Fateh. Fatima Barnawi is a black Palestinian woman, born in Jerusalem in 1939, who spent most of her childhood in a refugee camp in Amman, Jordan. In the 1960s, she joined Fateh and took part in a military operation in Jerusalem in 1967, just after the Six Day War. She was arrested and gaoled for life by the Israelis. In 1977, she was released in a prisoner exchange and continued to be active in the resistance movement and in Fateh (Banat, 2018).

Shadia Abu-Ghazaleh was born in Nablus in 1947 and joined Fateh just after the Naksa. She was martyred in October 1968 at the age of 21 (PLO, 1975). Muzna Nicola was a trained nurse who returned to Palestine from Britain in 1975. She joined Fateh before being arrested by the Israelis for the 'crime' of recruiting people to Fateh in Nazareth. Dala Mughrabi was another qualified nurse who was brought up in the Sabra camp in Beirut. She joined Fateh and, in March 1978, led eleven fighters in a seaborne landing near Tel Aviv, in what was known as the Operation of the Martyr Kamal Adwan. The unit hijacked two buses as they attempted to get to the Israeli Knesset. Mughrabi raised the Palestinian flag and declared a 'free Palestinian homeland' before the unit became embroiled in a bloody battle with Israeli forces. Thirty-eight Israelis were killed, as were nine of the Palestinian militants, including Mughrabi (Khalili, 1977).

But not all the women activists were Fateh members. Perhaps the most famous of all women fighters is Leila Khaled. Khaled was brought up in a refugee camp in Damascus and joined the PFLP. She was a member of a PFLP unit that highjacked a TWA plane in 1969. The plane was diverted to Damascus, where it was blown up. Khaled had plastic surgery, changed her looks and then took part in another hijacking, though this one failed (Irving, 2012). She was just one of a number of women active in the PFLP. Others included Abla Taha, Latifa Howari and Sarah Joudeh, who were all arrested during 1968 and subjected to torture inside Israel's prisons (PLO, 1975)

Yet to focus on those women directly involved in the armed struggle should not allow us to lose sight of the vast numbers of women who have been involved in a range of resistance activities. Alsaafin (2014) notes an example from 1893, when "in the town of Afula...women demonstrated against the construction of a new [European] Jewish Settlement". Khaleq (2015) stresses that "Palestinian women have always been on the frontlines... During the British Mandate era in Palestine, the English shelled the village of Baqa al-Gharbiyeh in 1936. The army then took all the men of the village prisoner. The women responded by descending upon the military barracks at night with their children, armed only with rocks, demanding the army's release of their men, which they succeeded in achieving".

Historically, a vast range of grassroots organisations, which today might be termed civil society organisations, have been involved in the broad-based national liberation struggle, and women have actively engaged in these highly political networks and structures.

In 1929 the Arab Women's Union was set up, after nine women were killed whilst protesting in Jerusalem. The Union was involved in a range of social, economic and political campaigns which included organizing protests and demonstrations.

In 1933 two sisters in Yafa, Moheeba and Arabiya Khursheed, set up an organization called Zahrat al-Uqhawan (the Chrysanthemum Flowers) (Alsaafin, 2014). This group originally started as a campaigning welfare network, but after Moheeda witnessed a young Palestinian boy being shot by British forces, they turned themselves into an armed resistance organization. During the Nakba:

> The women in this organization provided invaluable medical services, carried food, water and ammunition to the rebels, dug trenches and erected barricades...[and] performed heroically in battle. (PLO, 1975: p7)

After 1948, women played a key role in creating and establishing a range of welfare networks to support refugees, including radical and popular social work organisations. According to PLO records, these included amongst others The Arab Child Welfare House, The Arab Women's Society, The Young Arab Women's Club and The Association for the Support of Wounded Militants. Such groups provided immediate support to meet people's needs but also had an educative and campaigning role within the refugee diaspora.

After the Naksa of 1967, women also came to the fore in the protest movements erupting across the West Bank and Gaza. As Alsaafin notes:

> Women joined the Palestinian resistance factions and engaged in political work... [W]hether in armed resistance, social work or in secret organizational work. (Alsaafin, 2014)

Women led several high-profile protest events. In January 1969, for example, women staged a sit-down strike in front of Israeli detention centres across the West Bank demanding the release of their fathers, husbands, brothers and sons. In Jerusalem, twelve Palestinian women held a three-day sit-in occupation of the Church of the Holy Sepulchre. The following month, in Gaza, between 2,000 and 3,000 girls from three girls' high schools fought a pitched battle with occupying forces, whilst schoolgirls from the Al-Zahra Secondary School protested outside the courts in Gaza at the trial of three women, chanting the slogan 'We are all fedayeen' (PLO, 1975: pp10,11).

However, it was the First Intifada that witnessed a more significant involvement by women in the liberation struggle.

Particularly important were the Women's Action Committees, a decentralized network operating across Palestine48, that encouraged local leaderships and local initiatives as part of the movement. This allowed women in Gaza, or in the North of the West Bank in Nablus, Jenin and Tulkarem and more remote villages, to play a part in the movement. The women:

> Participated in civil disobedience...sheltered youth and defied soldiers...participated in distributing secret communiques, delivered...funds for social relief, visited prisoners and their families. (James, 2013: p19)

They were involved in the mass protests, strikes, alternative education centres and health and welfare networks established to meet people's needs. They were active across Palestine48 and were fighting for national liberation and for a reinvigorated and prominent role for women in public and social life.

In response they were harried, imprisoned and tortured by the Israelis.

Since 1967, over 10,000 women have been arrested by the Israelis for their political activity (Asaafin, 2014), a clear indication of their significance and importance in the struggle for liberation.

In some poems, Tuqan celebrated the activities of these brave young men and women who engaged in direct conflict with the colonizing power. During the First Intifada, she wrote 'Martyrs of the Intifada', describing the young heroic stone-throwers of the uprising:

> They died standing, blazing on the road
> Shining like stars, their lips pressed to the lips of life
> They stood up in the face of death
> Then disappeared like the sun.

She starts her autobiography with her poem 'Song of Becoming' and in the afterword she notes:

> I have written one poem which totally fits the Intifada; 'Song of Becoming'... I wrote it after the June War in 1967, and

you can see how prophetic it is! It describes the Intifada before it started, which proves how absolutely inevitable it was; it is the essential response to the fact of occupation. (Tuqan, 1985: p204)

The poem speaks of the young resistance fighters who are forced to grow up quickly:

They're only boys
who used to frolic and play
releasing in the Western wind
their blue red green kites
the colour of the rainbow
jumping, whistling, exchanging spontaneous jokes
and laughter
fencing with branches, assuming the roles
of great heroes in history

But now these young children have "grown suddenly now/ grown more than the years of a lifetime" and in the process they have taken on a responsibility to resist, to tear down oppressive structures and to rebuild a free Palestine:

They're now the voice that rejects
They're the dialectics of destruction and building anew

Here is her clear recognition that the future rests with a new generation of fighters, they are:

The anger burning on the fringes of a blocked horizon
Invading classrooms, streets, city quarters
Centring on the squares
And facing sullen tanks with a stream of stones.
                    (Tuqan, 1985 p10)

In the second volume of her autobiography, *A More Difficult Journey* (1993), she wrote about the Intifada stating:

People who live the realities of death every day, every hour; children who have been robbed of their youth; the young men who want to reclaim their future are confronting Israeli military forces that are armed with tanks. Their weapons are just rocks and patriotism, and an indomitable will to resist.

The Intifada is the most significant event in the struggle between the Arabs and the Israelis. The final goal is to become free of Israeli occupation, to be free of the repression and inequality and to recover freedom and human dignity. (in Song, 2008: p31)

But she also wrote poems that were an affirmation of Palestinian identity and of the dream of return, even if that return should happen after death. In 'Enough For Me', Tuqan depicts herself as a link in the chain of history:

I ask nothing more
Than to die in my country
To dissolve and merge with the grass,
To give life to a flower
That a child of my country will pick,

All I ask
Is to remain in the bosom of my country
As soil,
Grass,
A flower.

(Tuqan, 1985 p231)

When I first read this poem, I was reminded of the Italian partisan anthem 'Bella Ciao', where the narrator asks his beloved that if he should die fighting the fascists, he be buried in the mountains, under the shade of a beautiful flower; "the flower of the partisan" and a symbol of resistance, belonging and steadfastness.

Towards the end of her life during the Second Intifada, Tuqan was living under curfew in Nablus. During this time, she wrote 'Longing: Inspired by the Law of Gravity'. She is bedridden and contemplates her isolation, locked down under curfew without friends and family to "fill the house with laughter", living alone with her shadow.

The tragic irony is that Tuqan, by this stage of her life, finds herself isolated and restricted within her home in Nablus, like the young girl she describes in *A Mountainous Journey*. But here, of course, the curfew is imposed by the Israelis.

The poem starts by emphasizing the stillness and isolation of the home:

Time's out and I'm home alone with the shadow I cast

…

No father, no mother
No brothers, no sisters to swell
The house full with laughter
Nothing but loneliness and grief

She moves on to list the simple things that she misses that make life bearable:

I miss the smell of coffee, the scent in the air… I miss the company of books… I miss, how I miss my mother's ancient clock, family photos framed on the wall/I miss my oud.

But importantly, these are not listed as things we inevitably lose as we come towards the end of our lives; these are pains inflicted by siege and curfew:

Time's out and I'm home alone
The curfew hurts
It hurts me, no it kills me…

The poem ends with a contemplation of death:

I'm afraid of tomorrow
I'm afraid of the unknowable resources of fate
O God, don't let me be a burden, shunned by young and old
I wait to arrive where the land is silent, I'm waiting for death
Long has been my journey O God
Make the path short and the journey end

Tuqan's art combined the personal and the political. It emphasized that the struggle for a free Palestine had to be part of a broader struggle for individual freedom and, crucially, that struggle had to include the liberation of women across the region. She stands out as a great woman poet of the Palestinian revolution.

Chapter 6
Voice of the poor: Naji al-Ali *

"I am not neutral, I am on the side of the poor" (Naji al-Ali)

THIS FINAL CHAPTER turns to explore the work of the Arab caricaturist Naji al-Ali. Al-Ali was a prolific artist, producing somewhere in the region of 40,000 drawings between the mid-1960s and the mid-1980s. They were published in Lebanon, Kuwait, the UAE and London and appeared in books, newspapers and at exhibitions. The cartoons themselves are deceptively simple line drawings in black and white, but the caricatures are powerful and easily understood by a mass audience.

His work forces us to confront questions of class, poverty and the role of Arab ruling classes in abandoning, or betraying, the Palestinians. Central to his work was a focus on the refugee communities in the Palestinian diaspora. As Fayad notes, because of the Nakba:

> Millions of Palestinian refugees...were forced to flee their homes to [go to] neighboring Arab countries including Lebanon, Syria, and Jordan. Little did they know that becoming refugees would not only lead to the loss of their homeland but also to the denial of their basic human rights in countries they cannot even call home. (Fayad, 2018)

* For copyright reasons, we have not reproduced any of al-Ali's full cartoons here. But many of his cartoons are available to view on the internet. Simply type in Handala or Naji al-Ali and you will soon get access to hundreds of images. Over 100 of his cartoons are available to view on the Handala website (http://www.handala.org/cartoons/index.html), which is divided into sections covering various themes including Arab Regimes, Women, Refugees, Resistance, Oil, Israel and the USA. And there is an excellent collection of his cartoons, with an introduction by Joe Sacco in *A Child In Palestine: The Cartoons of Naji al-Ali* published by Verso.

Seven decades after the Nakba, Palestinian refugees remain in impoverished camps across the Middle East. Their future remains uncertain but they remain focused on their 'right to return' to their homes and lands from which they were ethnically cleansed in 1947/48. One of their greatest advocates was al-Ali and today, over 30 years after his murder, his cartoons continue to inspire thousands in the camps.

Al-Ali was part of a longer Arabic tradition of political cartoonists who established a place for themselves in the increasing number of Arabic newspapers that developed over the twentieth century. The cartoons in the newspapers were not for decorative purposes. Tobocman suggests they were:

> deeply didactic. It is the job of the cartoonist to explain complex political problems in such a way that the simplest person can understand them. The artist deploys an arsenal of well-understood symbols that speak to the history of the nation. He tries to combine them in new ways to describe a continually changing contemporary situation. But this is more than an intellectual exercise. This is a form of militant activism. (Tobocman, 2017: pix)

Al-Ali was a hugely popular cartoonist within this broader Arabic tradition.

Naji al-Ali was born in 1937 in the village of al-Shajara, between Nazareth and Tiberias in the Eastern Gallilee. At the age of ten, his family had to flee when al-Shajara was destroyed and 'cleansed' by the Golani Brigade on 7 May 1948 (Pappe, 2006: p88).

The family fled to Southern Lebanon and al-Ali grew up in the Ain al-Hilweh refugee camp. Ain al-Hilweh is the largest of sixteen Palestinian camps in Lebanon and is situated just south-east of the city of Saida, approximately half-way between Tyre and Beirut. Today, Ain al-Hilweh remains an overcrowded, poverty stricken home to over 55,000 people (Suleiman, 2006: p8). Al-Ali later recalled that:

> I was a child of ten when we came to Ain al-Hilweh

refugee camp. We were hungry, dazed and barefoot. Life in the camp was unbearable, full of daily humiliation, ruled by poverty and despair. (Elkhalfaoui, 2018)

In 1950 there were an estimated 127,600 Palestinian refugees in Lebanon. By the turn of the century this had grown to just over 400,000 (Suleiman, 2006: p6).

As Ibrahim notes, the "Palestinian refugee camps in Lebanon are widely recognized as having the worst living conditions of any of the Palestinian refugee camps" (Ibrahim, 2008: p83). The Lebanese government primarily left the social and economic needs of the Palestinians to UNWRA and, at least until 1968, saw the Palestinians as a security threat. The refugees were defined not as refugees, with internationally recognized rights, but as a 'special category of foreigner', without rights.

As such, Palestinian refugees in Lebanon were excluded from jobs, public education and health services. Legally, they were not allowed to acquire, transfer or inherit property. They were denied access to Social Security and had to obtain a work permit before they could access unskilled jobs; skilled jobs were denied to Palestinians under a decree of 1962 which listed jobs and trades which could only be occupied by Lebanese nationals.

This was the situation until the Cairo Agreement of 1968. This agreement signed between Yasar Arafat, on behalf of the Palestinians, and General Emile Bustani, on behalf of the Lebanese government, allowed control over the sixteen Palestine refugee camps in Lebanon to pass from the Lebanese Armed Forces to the PLO.

The agreement started to unravel during the Lebanese civil war from 1975 onwards and was formally declared null and void by the Lebanese parliament in 1987, leaving Palestinian refugees in Lebanon a discriminated and marginalized community in the country.

Al-Ali grew up and lived in the camps in Lebanon during the 1950s and 1960s. Experiences of poverty, discrimination and displacement would shape his life, his politics and his cultural output. Artist Joe Sacco quotes him as saying: "As soon as I was aware of what was going on, all the havoc in our region, I felt I had to contribute somehow" (Sacco, 2009: pviii)

He gained an elementary education at a Christian school in Sidon, obtaining his leaving certificate in 1951, then worked for a short period picking oranges and olives before moving to Tripoli, in the north of the country, to train as a motor mechanic. In 1953 he moved to Beirut, where he worked in several small industrial workshops, then in 1957 he moved to Saudi Arabia for work. In 1959 he returned to Beirut and the following year he enrolled in the Lebanese Academy of Fine Arts.

By now al-Ali had begun to engage with the Arab Nationalist Movement and attended meetings and distributed pamphlets. This brought him to the attention of the Lebanese secret police and he was regularly picked up and imprisoned. As he notes: "during that time, I was arrested and imprisoned six or seven items" (al-Ali n.d.). Because of this harassment and the fact he was running out of money, he left the academy.

He was arrested in 1961 in Lebanon and spent 25 days in prison as a political prisoner. It was during his detention that he began to draw more seriously:

> Like others in the camp, I felt a need to express myself, to take part in protest demonstrations, to participate in national events, to subject myself like others to mistreatment and prison. At that point in my life, I developed a strong desire to draw. I began to try to express my political attitudes, my anxiety and my grief through paintings on the walls. I always made sure I had my pen with me when I was taken to prison. (al-Ali n.d.)

Just after his release from his 25-day detention, he was involved in setting up an exhibition of paintings in the Ain al-Hilweh camp. Ghassan Kanafani happened upon the exhibition and saw his work and commissioned two drawings for his *al-Hurriyya* (Freedom) magazine in 1962. Al-Ali was now on the road to becoming a professional cartoonist.

Across the refugee camps, graffiti is used to get simple messages and instructions out to the community. This would take on a particularly important role during the First Intifada, when calls for strikes or demonstrations were painted onto the walls of people's homes or onto communal spaces. In the camps there is a sense that whilst the inside of people's homes are their own, the outside walls are communal spaces where graffiti, posters, political slogans or martyr posters can be put up.

Drawing simple cartoons or graffiti on walls became an accessible medium that allowed al-Ali to make political points and ask political questions in a way that was easily understood.

His cartoons are full of social and political criticism.

He used his drawings to expose the reality of inequality and poverty; of political corruption, the misuse of power and lack of accountability; of Arab collusion with imperialism and the marginalisation and silencing of Palestinian refugees. He castigated the Arab ruling classes, especially in the Gulf, for their obedience to Western powers. He ridiculed political leaders and uncovered the pretence and hypocrisy of the rich. He was merciless in his criticism of American imperialism and, of course, of Israel.

As Najjar puts it:

> Al-Ali spared no-one: dictatorial Arab regimes, "Petrodollar-Arabs", Iranian leader Khomeini, the PLO bureaucracy that had grown inefficient, Yasser Arafat's official biographer, Palestinian upper-class pretensions, Arab Americans he considered soft on American Middle East policy, the US government's thirst for oil and its uncritical support for Israeli excesses, and of course the Israeli occupation of Lebanon in the 1980s and of the West Bank and Gaza. (Najar, 2007: p258)

With Kanafani's help, al-Ali moved to Kuwait in 1962 to work on the paper *Al-Tali'a al-Kuwaitiya* (The Kuwaiti Forward), published by the Kuwaiti Progressive Party. He later claimed that the relative freedom he had in Kuwait allowed him to grow as a political cartoonist.

149

In 1966 he returned to Lebanon, where he worked for almost a year as an illustrator on the magazine *al-Hurriyya* (Freedom) and the daily *al-Yawm* (The Day).

But like many Arab nationalists and leftists within the Palestinian community, it was the events of the June 1967 war that would change al-Ali's political direction.

In a letter dated 5 June, 1967, Naji al-Ali announced the birth of his most famous character: Handala. Now back in Kuwait, the letter explained that Handala's mother was named Al Nakba,

and he possessed no identity card nor held any nationality. But he made a promise: "I am Handala from the Ain al-Hilweh camp. I give my word of honor that I'll remain loyal to the cause..." (Al-Ali n.d.)

The name Handala comes from the Arabic word Handhal, which is a bitter tasting plant. The name was attached to a Palestinian child, embittered by the humiliating and cruel life forced on the refugees. The child was 10 years old (al-Ali's age when he was forced to leave Palestine) and would not grow older until he could return to his homeland.

His hair is unkempt and jagged like thorns ready to prick the oppressor. His feet are bare and his clothes are rags, like those of the children of the camps.

His hands are firmly clasped behind his back because he will not offer his hand to those who have put him in this position and because he is rejecting the various attempts at 'peace.' Or perhaps, as Sacco (2009) suggests, it is a pose that emphasises that he is inspecting, watching and recording events.

In some early cartoons, Handala's face can be seen, but after the Arab-Israeli War of 1973, Handala turns his back on the world as the world turned its back on Palestine. From this point, his back is turned away from the viewer, but he is there as a knowing witness to the horrors inflicted on the Palestinians. As al-Ali himself described him:

> This child, as you can see, is neither beautiful, spoiled, nor even well-fed. He is barefoot like many children in refugee camps. Those who came to know 'Hanthala,' as I discovered later, adopted him because he is affectionate, honest, outspoken, and a bum. He is an icon that stands to watch me from slipping. And his hands behind his back are a symbol of rejection of all the present negative tides in our region. (in El Fassed, 2004)

Handala is a symbol of steadfastness, of resilience and of resistance. From this moment he appears in almost every al-Ali cartoon, taking the place of al-Ali's signature.

Handala is also a partisan figure. Al-Ali understood that, overwhelmingly, the victims of the Israeli occupation and ethnic cleansing are the poor and the dispossessed. It is refugees who suffer, who are sent to jail and who die. In his short autobiographical essay, he argues:

> I am from Ain al-Hilweh, a camp like any other camp. The people of the camps were the people of the land in Palestine. They were not merchants or landowners. They were farmers. When they lost their land, they lost their lives. The bourgeoisie never had to live in the camps, whose inhabitants were exposed to hunger, to every degradation and to every form of oppression. Entire families died in our camps. (al-Ali n.d.)

And he asserts: "I am accused of being biased, and I don't deny it. I am not neutral; I am on the side of the poor" (Elkhalfaoui, 2018).

But Handala also became an anchor, tethering al-Ali to his roots in Palestine and maintaining his connection to the refugee experience. Handala had a knowing view of the world and its treatment of Palestinians, but he also had an eye on al-Ali

ensuring he held true to the spirit of the Palestinian revolution.
As al-Ali put it:

> The character of Handala was a sort of icon that protected
> my soul from falling whenever I felt sluggish or I was
> ignoring my duty. That child was like a splash of fresh water
> on my forehead, bringing me to attention and keeping
> me from error and loss. He was the arrow of the compass,
> pointing steadily towards Palestine. (al-Ali n.d.)

There are other recurring figures in al-Ali's cartoons.

Fatima wears a traditional Palestinian embroidered dress. On her head is a hijab and, very often, around her neck is a key. The key is important for Palestinians as a symbol of the 'right of return'. This itself is the key to establishing real peace in a democratic and secular Palestine. The embroidered dress ties Fatima to Palestine; the dress designs vary across Palestine48 with local trees, flora and fauna woven into the pattern to identify the region the wearer is from. Fatima's short dress sleeves indicate she is a peasant woman, used to working the land. Thus, she represents a connection to the land and to home. She appears as a symbol of steadfastness, always there, encouraging others not to give up the fight but to continue with the struggle. She is wise and a universal figure of Palestinian womanhood and goodness.

Here is a section of a cartoon showing the man, or the good man. His patched clothes emphasising his poverty and his status as a refugee.

Al-Zalama (the man) is a representative of the poor and refugees. He is poorly dressed, like Handala, and his clothes are rags. He is often found hard at work and confronting the harshness of life in the camps. Or he appears, pointedly, when refugee voices have been silenced by their so-called betters or leaders. He is there when there is yet another injustice inflicted on refugees as a result of some deal made by Arab leaders with the Americans or the Israelis. His voice is ignored and he is side-lined and marginalized, but he is the constant presence of the refugee poor, demanding his right to return home and live in peace and with dignity.

In this section of a cartoon, you see an example of a wealthy Palestinian. He makes money from turning Palestinian goods, like the keffiyeh, into commercial artefacts. In the background is a fighter with the headscarf as it should be worn!

Here is an example of a fat, wealthy member of the Arab elite who is always ready to sell out the Palestinians.

Finally, there are the 'Evil men' who appear in the cartoons, who are usually drawn fat, sometimes with bodies that resemble slugs. These men have the trappings of wealth and power and live the good life, happy to exploit the Palestinian catastrophe for their own ends. Here is the Arab quisling, the bureaucrat, the apparatchik, the flashy businessman or member of the Arab elite. They are often seen taking Palestinian symbols, like the keffiyeh, and turning them into harmless fashion statements to schmooze the globally powerful. A target for some of al-Ali's ire, here are wealthy Palestinians in the diaspora living 'the high life' whilst others are left in impoverished camps.

Al-Ali also uses common Christian and Muslim symbols.

Christ often appears in al-Ali's cartoons. Sometimes he is on the cross with a key around his neck, or he has barbed wire replacing the crown of thorns, and at other times he wears a simple keffiyeh. On occasions, he can be seen removing his nailed hands or feet from the cross to throw a stone at or kick Israeli guards. The message is clear: al-Ali is using common, known symbols to draw parallels between the suffering of Christ and that of contemporary Palestinians.

On another occasion, al-Ali shows al-Zalama and Handal on Pilgrimage to Mecca. During Hajj, pilgrims are meant to wear the same white cloth, showing that in front of god they are all equal. But al-Zalama wears the black of mourning and Handala's clothes are his usual darned rags. The other pilgrims wear sandals, but both Handala and al-Zamala are barefoot. The pilgrims from the Gulf are fat but the two Palestinians are emaciated. Here we have al-Ali questioning the message of equality between Muslims and forcing readers to consider the plight of the refugees.

Some of al-Ali's most biting cartoons deal with the Arab elite, cow-towing to US interests and remaining silent about the US role in the region.

This section of one of his cartoons shows Arab leaders keeping  silent to win favour with the Americans.

Al-Ali spent his time moving between Lebanon and Kuwait. In the late 1960s and 1970s, Kuwait was becoming increasingly important to the US because of its oil resources. Al-Ali's connections in both countries helped him come to a clearer understanding of the imperial dynamic at play in the region and the Middle East's importance as an oil resource and strategic outpost in the Cold War era. These drawings meant that al-Ali cartoons—and Handala—became more universal. As he notes:

At first he [Handala] was a Palestinian child, but his consciousness developed to have a national then a global and human horizon. He is a simple yet tough child, and this is why people adopted him and felt that he represents their consciousness. (Al-Ali n.d.)

There are numerous cartoons that combine images of Israeli bombs with US-marked oil drums or show images of US soldiers literally beating the 'drums of war' on oil drums, or of the stars and stripes strangling Arab populations. Alongside these are images of Arab leaders consciously silent about the destruction of Arab lands and of Palestinian hopes of return.

Some of his angriest and most moving drawings deal with the Israeli invasion of Lebanon in 1982. Al-Ali was in Lebanon during the Israeli offensive. He drew pictures that captured the horror of death and destruction at Israeli hands. Several cartoons depict in a moving way the massacres of Sabra and Shatila. One such image has Handala using a keffiyeh to cover the brutalized body of a young Palestinian woman. Another has two orphaned children standing in a cemetery with flowers in their hands, a Palestinian keffiyeh symbolically being wrapped around one of the children to keep her safe.

But the war in Lebanon and the long-running Lebanese civil war also saw various Arab regimes interfere in Lebanese politics, make agreements with the Israeli invaders and arm their own factions within the Palestinian camps. They did these things to promote their own interests at the expense of Palestinian unity and the aims of the Liberation Movement. Al-Ali argued that when he returned to Lebanon in the early 1980s, the atmosphere in the camps had changed:

> the camp was an armed jungle, but it lacked political clarity. It had been divided into tribes. Various Arab regimes had invaded it and Arab oil dollars had corrupted many of its young. The camp was a womb that generated true freedom fighters, but the outsiders were trying to stop that process... The Arab regimes committed crimes against us and against the Palestinian revolution itself. These circumstances explain much of what happened during the Israeli invasion of Lebanon. (al-Ali n.d.)

Al-Ali's cartoons lampooned the powerful and, especially after the Lebanese civil war, they included the leadership of the Palestinian Liberation Organisation and their supporters. He castigated the PLO for abandoning the refugees in Lebanon and for seeking avenues for peace or, as he saw it, capitulation with the Israelis. These were brave cartoons and uncompromising, but they made him enemies within the Palestinian camp.

His principled attacks on the Arab elite marked him out as a wanted man by many establishment figures.

His merciless and ruthless criticism of the Israelis meant he was hated by the Zionist regime, and by the mid-1980s he had many enemies on many sides. Throughout his life he received over 100 significant death threats.

After the Israeli assault of 1982, he moved back to Kuwait but, as a marked man, he fled, fearing Phalangist threats on his life. From 1983 he worked at the *Al-Qabas* (The Light) newspaper, the largest independent daily newspaper in the Middle East.

From Kuwait he continued to publish cartoons lampooning the Arab ruling classes and speaking truth to power. In 1985 the Saudi regime put pressure on the Kuwaitis and al-Ali was forced out of Kuwait, taking his family to live in London, though he continued to work for *Al-Qabas*.

On 22 July, 1987, he was shot in the head by a gunman as he left the *Al-Qabas* offices in London. He was in a coma for five weeks, dying on Saturday 30 August. He was just 49. The assassin has never been found.

But whilst the assassin took al-Ali's life, he could not eradicate Handala.

Across the Middle East, where people struggle for freedom, Handala makes an appearance. He is on walls and posters across the West Bank and Gaza. He was a symbol of the Arab Spring as it sprung into life and he appeared in Tahrir Square during the height of the Egyptian uprising. He continues to be a symbol of hope and freedom as the oppressed across the Middle East continue to fight for a better world.

Conclusion:
The continuing relevance of the 'rocks in the valley'

KANAFANI, DARWISH, TUQAN AND AL-ALI were great Palestinian cultural figures from the high point of what is called the era of 'national resistance literature', broadly dated as running between the 1960s and the early 1990s. This period starts with the growing dominance of Fatah within the PLO and ends with the signing of the Oslo Accords.

The work of the four flourished because it was embedded within the movement for Palestinian liberation. It grew out of, reflected and projected the demands, needs and perspectives of the Palestinian people. All four provide a Palestinian perspective on the disaster of expulsion, of colonial settlement and of oppression. They all capture something of the lived experience of the refugees and the dispossessed. Each exposes the brutality of the Israeli state and disastrous impact of global imperialism in the region. Each shines a spotlight on the betrayal of the Palestinians by Arab leaders.

Whilst al-Ali's cartoons can be viewed as didactic, this is simply not the case with the work of Kanafani, Darwish or Tuqan. The work of the three writers is written and presented in open and accessible forms. It uses ordinary and common images and well-known historic refence points that emphasise the connection of the people to the land and the common humanity of the Palestinians. But it also challenges the present, the structures of inequality and oppression that shape Palestinian lives.

It is important to emphasise that the cultural output of the four is not merely of historical interest. Part of the greatness of their art arises from the fact that it continues to speak to the lived experience of Palestinian communities. It still forces us to confront questions about Palestinian rights, freedom, and liberation. It challenges the hypocrisy of the powerful as they turn a blind eye to Israeli atrocities. And it goes beyond Palestinian specificities to speak to the plight of the poor and dispossessed across the globe.

In what remains of the conclusion I want to provide what might be called a guide to sources. That is, an oversight of where the works of the four can be found. I would urge people to read and engage with their work.

So, here is a brief overview of what to read and where to get it!

Ghasan Kanafani's 'Letter from Gaza' is freely available at the Marxist Internet Archive (available here: *https://www.marxists. org/archive/kanafani/1956/letterfromgaza.htm*). But as well as reading it, I strongly recommend watching John Berger read the letter from the 2008 Palestine Festival of Literature (available here: *https://youtu.be/lqmUqwl5d7U*).

There are three collections of his short stories available in English. *Men in the Sun and Other Stories* (1999) includes 'The Land of Sad Oranges', 'Umm Saad' and, of course, 'Men in the Sun'. *Palestine's Children: Returning to Haifa and Other Stories* (2000) includes several Umm Saad stories, and the important *Returning to Haifa. All That's Left to You: A novella and short stories* (2004) includes the title story plus a range of other stories about Palestinian life.

Mahmoud Darwish wrote a huge amount of poetry during his life. Many of his poems have been put to music and you can search for them on YouTube. If you search the internet, sites like *PoemHunter.com* will bring up a selection of Darwish's work. There are other websites that contain his poetry, and a quick search will lead you to some of his work.

A growing number of volumes of poetry are available in English. *Memory for Forgetfulness, August, Beirut, 1982* has been published by University of California Press and is a fantastic piece of writing. 'Journal of Ordinary Grief', 'In the Presence of Absence' and 'Why Did You Leave the Horses Alone?' are autobiographical poems well worth reading. His last poems are available in *A River Dies of Thirst*.

The poems appear in numerous anthologies. *Victims of a Map* (Adonis et al, 2005), *The Anthology of Modern Palestinian Literature* (Jayyusi, 1992) and *A Map of Absence* (Alshaer, 2019) are amongst the best.

Finally, if you are ever in Ramallah, visit the Darwish Museum (you might spend an hour or so there) on Al Ayyam Street. You should also aim to take in the Palestinian National Museum on Museum Street, off Omar Ibn Al-Khattab Street (and give yourself a good three hours). Both are easy to get to by taxi from the Al-Manara Square (or Lion's Square) in the centre of the city, which is on the main Jerusalem/Ramallah bus route.

Fadwa Tuqan's work is less easily accessible in English. The first volume of her autobiography, *A Mountainous Journey*, is essential reading. The autobiography ends with several of her poems. *PoemHunter.com* and similar sites will bring up some of her work, though they tend to be the same few poems in English. The Tuqans' home in Nablus is currently under reconstruction. The Old City in Nablus was badly destroyed during the Second Intifada and the local authorities are trying to turn her home into an appropriate museum. It is not yet open.

Naji al-Ali published cartoons in a range of publications. Some of these have been pulled together in a collection published by Verso called *A Child in Palestine* (2009). A large number of his cartoons can be viewed on the *Handala.org* website. Al-Ali is buried in London at the Islamic Brookwood Cemetery.

160

References

Abd Al-salam Ahmad, A.M. (2016) "Aspects of Ecofeminism in the Poetry of Fadwa Tuqan and Linda Hogan" Fayoum University Occasional Papers Vol 62 https://opde.journals.ekb.eg/article_86792_5f8eb255ace26c330df29599abf95550.pdf

Abu Eid, M. (2016) Mahmoud Darwish: Literature and the Politics of Palestinian Identity (London, IB Taurus)

Abu Nimah, H. (2005) Defusing Israel's "demographic bomb", The Electronic Intifada 8 March https://electronicintifada.net/content/defusing-israels-demographic-bomb/5503

Adonis, Darwish, M. and Al-Qasim, S. (2005) Victims of a Map: a bilingual anthology of Arabic poetry (new edition) (London, Al-Saqi books)

Agazi, Y. (1993) "I knew that one day I would join the struggle" Ha'aretz 16 July

Ahmad, A., M., A., A. (2017) "Aspects of Ecofeminism in the Poetry of Fadwa Tuqan and Linda Hogan" International Journal of Linguistics, Literature and Culture (LLC) Vol.4 No.2 http://ijllc.eu/wp-content/uploads/2019/01/Aspects-of-Ecofeminism-in-the-Poetry-of-Fadwa-Tuqan-and-Linda-Hogan.pdf#:~:text=Ecofeminism%20in%20Fadwa%20Tuqan%E2%80%99s%20Poetry%20Fadwa%20Tuqan,%20a,the%20ultimate%20deposition%20of%20Palestinians%20from%20their%20motherland.

Ahmed, H. Y., Hashim, R. S., Lazim, Z. M. and Vengadasamy, R. (2012) "Identity and Land in Mahmoud Darwish's Selected Poems: An Ecopostcolonial Reading" International Journal of Applied Linguistics and English Literature Vol 1, No 6 November pp7-19

al-Ali, N. (n.d.) "I am from Ain al-Helwa": Through the eyes of a Palestinian Child http://www.handala.org/about/iam.html

Algaz, Y. (1993) "I knew that one day I would join the struggle" Haartez 16 July

Alon, G. and Benn, A. (2003) "Netanyahu: Israel's Arabs Are the Real Demographic Threat" Haaretz !8 December https://www.haaretz.com/1.4802179

Alsaafin, L. (2014) "The role of Palestinian women in resistance" Open Democracy https://www.opendemocracy.net/en/north-africa-west-asia/role-of-palestinian-women-in-resistance/

Alshaer, A. (2019) *A Map of Absence: an anthology of Palestinian writing on the Nakba* (London,al-Saqi books)

al-Udhari, A. (2005) "Introduction" in Adonis, Darwish, M. and al-Quasimodo's *Victims of a Map: a bilingual anthology of Arabic poetry* (London, Saqi)

Al-Udhari, Abdullah (1984) "Mahmoud Darwish: Three poems" *Index on Censorship* 4/84 https://journals.sagepub.com/doi/pdf/10.1080/03064228408533756

American Muslims for Palestine (2012) "The Second Intifada" https://www.ampalestine.org/palestine-101/history/intifadas/second-intifada-introduction#:~:text=The%20Second%20Intifada%2C%20commonly%20referred%20to%20as%20the,to%20deprive%20Palestinians%20of%20their%20basic%20human%20rights.

Anderson, P. (2001) "Scurrying towards Bethlehem" *New Left Review* 10 July/August available at: http://newleftreview.org/A2330

Arafat, Y. (1974) Speech to the UN General Assembly, November. Available at: https://en.m.wikisource.org/wiki/Yasser_Arafat%27s_1974_UN_General_Assembly_speech

Asfour, J. M. (1988) *When the Words Burn: An anthology of modern Arabic poetry: 1945-1987.* Translated and edited by John Mikhail Asfour. Dunvegan, Ontario, Canada. Cormorant Books.

Ashrawi, H. M. (1978) "The contemporary Palestinian poetry of occupation" *Journal of Palestine Studies* Vol 7, Number 3 (Spring) pp77-101

Banat, B. Y. I (2018) "Palestinian women and resistance" *Anglisticum Journal* Volume 7: 3

Barr, J. (2012) *A Line in the Sand: Britain, France and the struggle that shaped the Middle East* (Simon and Schuster, London)

Ben-Sasson, H. H. (ed) (1985) *A History of the Jewish People* (Harvard, Harvard University Press). Excerpt available as "Jewish Emigration in the 19th Century" https://www.myjewishlearning.com/article/jewish-emigration-in-the-19th-century/

Berger, J. (2008) "Letter from Gaza", Palestine Festival of Literature 7-11 May https://youtu.be/lqmUqwl5d7U

Bitton, S. (1997) "Mahmoud Darwich: Et la terre, comme la langue" (Paris: France 3, Point du Jur [video])

Borger, J. (2017) "Donald Trump to recognise Jerusalem as Israel's capital and move US embassy" *The Guardian* 6 December https://www.theguardian.com/world/2017/dec/06/trump-recognise-jerusalem-israel-capital-move-us-embassy-white-house

Borger, J. (2019) "Trump says US will recognise Israel's sovereignty over Golan Heights" *The Guardian* 21 March https://www.theguardian.com/us-news/2019/mar/21/trump-us-golan-heights-israel-sovereignty

Brehony L. (2017) Ghassan Kanafani: Voice of Palestine (1936-1972) *Palestine*

162

Chronicle 4 September 2017. www.palestinechronicle.com/ghassan-Kanafani-voice-of-palestine-1936-1972/

Carleton, R. (1970) "PFLP: Ghassan Kanafani" *This Day Tonight* (ABC) https://youtu.be/3h_drCmG2iM

Carpenter, M. (2020) *Palestinian Popular Struggle* (London, Routledge)

Coffin, N. (1996) "Resistance in the Work of Ghassan Kanafani" *The Arab Studies Journal* Vol 4, No.2 pp98-118

Darwish, M. (1995) *Memory of Forgetfulness* (Berkeley, Uni of California Press)

Darwish, M. (2000) *The Adam of Two Edens: Selected poems* (New York, Syracuse University Press)

Darwish, M. (2009) *A River Dies of Thirst* (London SAQI)

Darwish, M. (2010) *Journal of Ordinary Grief* (New York, Archipelago books)

Darwish, M. (2010b) *State of Siege* (Syracuse, University Press)

Darwish, M. (2011) "To My Mother" *Palestine Advocacy Project*
https://www.palestineadvocacyproject.org/poetry-campaign/to-my-mother/#:~:text=%E2%80%9CTo%20My%20Mother%E2%80%9D%20is%20one%20of%20Darwish%E2%80%99s%20most,three%20things:%20his%20mother%E2%80%99s%20bread,%20coffee,%20and%20touch.

Darwish, M. (2012a) "A Soldier Dreams of White Lilies" (available at https://www.poemhunter.com/poem/a-soldier-dreams-of-white-lilies/)

Darwish, M. (2012b) "Rita and the Riffle" (available at https://www.poemhunter.com/poem/rita-and-the-rifle/)

Darwish, M. (2013/1986) *Memory for a Forgetfulness: August, Beirut, 1982* (university of California Press, London)

Defence for Children International (Palestine) (2018) "Year-in-Year Review: 2018 rained deadly force on Palestinian children" 31December https://www.dci-palestine.org/year_in_review_2018_reigned_deadly_force_on_palestinian_children

Defence for Children International (Palestine) [DCI(P)] (2020) "Israeli forces shoot and kill 15-year-old Palestinian boy" https://www.dci-palestine.org/israeli_forces_shoot_and_kill_15_year_old_palestinian_boy

El Fassed, A. (2004) "Naji al-Ali: The timeless conscience of Palestine" *The Electronic Intifada* 22 July https://electronicintifada.net/content/naji-al-ali-timeless-conscience-palestine/5166

Elkhalfaoui, A. (2018) "In Memoriam: Naji al-Ali, a Great Palestinian and Arab Cartoonist" *Inside Arabia: Voice of the Arab People* https://insidearabia.com/naji-al-ali-palestinian-arab-cartoonist/ (August)

Elmessiri, A. M. (1981) "The Palestinian Wedding: Themes of Contemporary Palestinian Resistance Poetry" *Journal of Palestine Studies* Vol 10, No. 3 (Spring) pp77-99

Fayad, A. (2018) "Discrimination of Palestinian Refugees in Lebanon" *Brown Political Review* 19 October https://brownpoliticalreview.org/2018/10/discrimination-of-palestinian-refugees-in-lebanon/

Fayyed, H. (2019) "Gaza's Great March of Return protests explained" *al-Jazeera* https://www.aljazeera.com/news/2019/03/gaza-great-march-return-protests-explained-190330074116079.html

Frankel, J. (1984). *Prophecy and Politics: Socialism, Nationalism, and the Russian Jews, 1862-1917*. (Cambridge, Cambridge University Press)

German, L. and Murray, Andrew (2005). *Stop the war: The story of Britain's biggest mass movement*. London: Bookmarks

Ghannam, M. and El-Zein, A (2009) "Reflecting on the life and work of Mahmoud Darwish" CIRS Brief, No 3. Centre for International and Regional Studies, Georgetown University

Gilmour, D. (1980) *Dispossessed: The ordeal of the Palestinians* (Sphere books, London)

Habash, G. (2008) *Les révolutionnaires ne meurent jamais: Conversations avec Georges Malbrunot*. (Paris: Fayard)

Hadawi, S. (1970) "Village Statistics of 1945: A classification of land and area ownership in Palestine" (Palestine Liberation Organization Research Center)

Halabi, Z. (2004) "Exclusion and identity in Lebanon's Palestinian refugee camps: a story of sustained conflict" *Environment and Urbanisation* Vol 16, No 2 (October 2004)

Hamdan, M., Zeyada, A. and A'teeq, L (2020) "The Father-Figure in Fadwa Tuqan's and Yael Dayan's Autobiographies" *International Journal of Linguistics, Literature and Translation*, Vol 3:6 pp156-164

Hamzah, H. (2014) "Resistance, Martyrdom and Death in Mahmoud Darwish's poetry" *Holy Land Studies* 13, 2 pp159-186

Harlow, B. (1987) *Resistance Literature* (New York, Methuen)

Hassan S. D. A. (2003) "Nation validation: Modern Palestinian Literature and the politics of appeasement" *Social Text* 75 (Vol 21, number 2) pp 7-23.

Hilmy, S. (2017) ""ID Card" by Mahmoud Darwish: A Translation and Commentary" *Washington Report on Middle East Affairs* (Nov-Dec) https://www.wrmea.org/017-november-december/id-card-by-mahmoud-darwish-a-translation-and-commentary.html

Hirst, D. (2003) *The Gun and the Olive Branch* (third edition) (London, Faber and Faber)

Hourani, A. (1991) *A History of the Arab Peoples* (London, Faber and Faber)

Ibrahim, J. (2008) The Discrimination Against Palestinian Refugees Living In Lebanon" *Palestine-Israel Journal of Politics, Economics and Culture* Vol 15 Issue 1,

164

pp83-90

Irving, S. (2012) *Leila Khaled: icon of Palestinian liberation* (London, Pluto)

Jaggi, M. (2002) "Poet of the Arab world" *The Guardian* 8 June 2002 https://www.theguardian.com/books/2002/jun/08/featuresreviews.guardianreview19

James, M. K. (2013) "Women and the Intifadas: the evolution of Palestinian Women's Organisations" *Strife Journal* Issue 1 (March) https://www.strifejournal.org/wp-content/uploads/2020/05/STRIFE_1_3_JAMES_M_18_22.pdf

Jarrar W. S. (2005) "Love And War In The Poetry of Fadwa Tuqan" *Al-Quds University Journal for Research and Studies* No.5 (March) https://dspace.qou.edu/bitstream/194/1710/1/577-2193-1-PB.pdf

Jayyusi, S. K. (1990) "Forward" to Tuqan, F *A Mountainous Journey* (Minnesota, Grey Wolf Press)

Jayyusi, S. K. (ed) (1992) *Modern Arabic Poetry: An Anthology* (Columbia University Press, New York)

Just World Educational (2019) "Palestinian Prisoners in Israel's Jails: Facts and resources" https://justworldeducational.org/2019/04/palestinian-prisoners-in-israels-jail-facts-and-resources/

Kanafani, A. (1973) *Ghassan Kanafani* (Palestine Research Centre, Beirut)

Kanafani, G. (1956) "Letter from Gaza" *Marxist Internet Archive* https://www.marxists.org/archive/kanafani/1956/letterfromgaza.htm

Kanafani, G. (1966) *Resistance Literature in Occupied Palestine (1948-66)* (Beirut: Dar AlAdab. reprinted, 2001 Ministry of Education,Baghdad)

Kanafani, G. (1972) *The 1936-39 Revolt in Palestine* (Committee for a Democratic Palestne, New York) available at www.kanan48.files.wordpress.com/2011/04/ghassan1.gif

Kanafani, G. (1999) *Men in the Sun and Other Palestinian Stories* (London, Rienner)

Kanafani, G. (2000) *Palestine's Children, Returning to Haifa and Other Stories* (London, Reiner)

Kanafani, G. (2004) *All That's Left to You: A novella and short stories* (London, Interlink Books)

Karpf, A. (2002) "Remember the pain, heal the wounds" *The Guardian* 26 March 2002 http://www.guardian.co.uk/world/2002/mar/26/israel1

Kayali, L. (2021) *Palestinian Women and Popular Resistance: Perceptions, attitudes and strategies* (London, Routledge)

Khaleq, E. (2015) "Palestinian women: the backbone of resistance" *Liberation School* (November) https://liberationschool.org/palestinian-women-the-backbone-of-resistance/

Khalili, G. (1977) *Palestinian Women and Revolution* (Beirut: PLO)

Khoury, E. (2013) "Remembering Ghassan Kanafani, or how a Nation was born of story telling" *Journal of Palestine Studies* Vol 42, No.3 pp85-91

King, T. (2011) Tawfiq Ziad, Israel and 'Unadikum' *Samuel-news* 15 May http://www.salem-news.com/articles/may152011/unidakum-tk.php

Klemm, V. (2000) "Different notions of commitment (Iltizam) and Committed Literature (al-adab al-multazim) in the literary circles of the Mashriq" *Arabic and Middle Eastern Literatures* Vol 3, No 1

Krystall, N. (1988) The de-Arabization of West Jerusalem 1947-1950 *Journal of Palestine Studies* 27 pp5-22

Kuttab, E. (2006) "The Palestinian Women's Movement: From Resistance and Liberation to Accommodation and Globalization" In: Vents d'Est, vents d'Ouest: Mouvements de femmes et féminismes anticoloniaux [online]. Genève: Graduate Institute Publications, 2009 (generated 30 avril 2019). Available on the Internet: http://books.openedition.org/iheid/6310

Langendorf, M. (2019) "House demolitions on the rise in East Jerusalem." *The Arab Weekly* 20/07/2019 https://thearabweekly.com/house-demolitions-rise-east-jerusalem

Magrath, D. R. "A study of "Rijal final-Shams" by Ghassan Kanafani" *Journal of Arabic Literature* Vol 10 pp95-108

Marx, K. (1867) Capital (Volume 1), chapter 31 *Marxist Internet Archive* https://www.marxists.org/archive/marx/works/1867-c1/ch31.htm

Masalha, N. (2018) *Palestine: A Four Thousand Year History* (London, Zed Books)

Mattawa, K. (2014) *Mahmoud Darwish: The poet's art and his nation* (New York, Syracuse University Press)

McCarthy, R. (2006) "Sisters, mothers, martyrs" *The Guardian* 5 December https://www.theguardian.com/world/2006/dec/05/gender.israel

Middle East Monitor (2019) "19 years after he was shot, Muhammad Al-Durrah's killers still walk free" *MEM* 30 September https://www.middleeastmonitor.com/20190930-19-years-after-he-was-shot-muhammad-al-durrahs-killers-still-walk-free/

Mir, S. (2013) "Palestinian Literature: Occupation and Exile" *Arab Studies Quarterly* Vol 35,2 (Spring) pp110-129

Moffett, G. (1988) "Israeli left finds words, like stones, can hurt" *Christian Science Monitor* 5 April https://www.csmonitor.com/1988/0405/olect.html

Morris, B. (2008) *1948: A history of the first Arab-Israeli War* (Yale University Press, New Haven)

Muhawi, I. (2013) "Introduction" in Darwish, M. (2013/1986) *Memory for a Forgetfulness: August, Beirut, 1982* (university of California Press, London)

Najjar, O. A. (2007) "Cartoons as a site for the construction of Palestinian refugee identity: an exploratory study of cartoonist Naji al-Ali" *Journal of Communication*

166

Inquiry Vol 31, No3 pp255-285

Nashef, H. A. M. (2016) "Challenging the myth of 'a land without a people':
Mahmoud Darwish's Journal of an Ordinary Grief and In the Presence of Absence"
The Journal of Commonwealth Literature, Vol 53, (3) pp394-411

Natour, R. (2020) "The Palestinian National Poet and the Silencing of Women's
Voices" *Haartez* 28/06/2020 https://www.haaretz.com/middle-east-news/.
premium-mahmoud-darwish-s-honor-is-silencing-palestinian-women-s-
voices-1.8953447

Neff, D. (1998) "Battle of Karameh establishes claim of Palestinian statehood"
Washington Report on Middle East Affairs, March 1998 pp87-88 (available at
https://www.wrmea.org/1998-march/middle-east-history-it-happened-in-march.
html)

Padel, R. (2009) "Preface" in *Mahmoud Darwish A River Dies of Thirst* (London,
SAQI books)

Pappe, I. (2006) *The Ethnic Cleansing of Palestine* (One world, Oxford)

Pedatzur, R. (2004) "More than a million bullets" *Haaretz* 29/6/04 http://www.
haaretz.com/hasen/pages/ShArt.jhtml?itemNo=444992

Peled, M. (1982) "Palestinian literature 1917-1948" *Arabica T.* 29 Fasc 2 (June)
pp143-183

PLO (1975) *The Struggle of Palestinian Women* (Beirut, PLO)

Rashid, M. (1970) "Towards a Democratic State in Palestine", PLO Research
Centre, Beirut

Riley, K. (2000) "Ghassan Kanafani: A biographical essay" in Kanafani, G. (2000)
Palestine's Children: Returning to Haifa and other stories (Reiner books, Colorado).

Rose, J. (1986) *Israel: The hijack state* (London, SWP)

Rosen, M. (1974) "The history of modern Palestine in Brief" in Kamal Boullata
(1974) *Palestine Lives! Songs from the struggle of the people of Palestine* (New
York: Paredon Records)

Sacco, J. (2009) "Introduction" in Naji al-Ali *A Child in Palestine* (London, Verso)

Said, E. W. (2000) *Reflections on Exile and other Literary and Cultural Essays*
(London, Granta)

Said, E. W. and Barsamian, D. (2003) *Culture and Resistance: Conversations with
Edward W. Said* Cambridge (Mass) South End Press.

Salih, R. and Richter-Devroe, S. (2014) "Cultures of resistance in Palestine and
Beyond: On the politics of Art, Aesthetics and affect" *The Arab Studies Journal* Vol
22, No 1 (spring) pp8-27

Sartre, J. P. (1947/1978) *What Is Literature?* Trans. Bernard Frechtman.
(Gloucester: Peter Smith)

Seal, J. (2017) "Land of the Three Faiths": The Little-known History of the

167

Palestinian Declaration of Independence. *Haaretz* (originally 27 Nov 2009; reprinted 15 November 2017) https://www.haaretz.com/middle-east-news/palestinians/the-1988-declaration-of-independence-1.5150321

Song, K. S. (2008) "A Crisis in Palestinian Literature: The Case of Fadwa Tuqan" *Japan Association for Middle East Studies Special* Issue II: The Perspectives of Arabic literature-Beyond the Areas and the Ages https://www.jstage.jst.go.jp/article/ajames/24/1/24_KJ00005075222/_pdf/-char/ja

Sorby, K. (2005) "Arab nationalism after the Young Turk Revolution (1908-1914)" *Asian and African Studies* 14,1 pp.4-21

Suleiman, J. (2006) "Marginalised community: The case of Palestinian Refugees in Lebanon" DRC Research Reports, Sussex, UK, DRC on Migration, Globalisation and Poverty https://assets.publishing.service.gov.uk/media/57a08c4be5274a31e0001112/JaberEdited.pdf

Swedenborg, T. (2003) *Memories of Revolt: The 1936-1939 Rebellion and the Palestinian National Past* (The University of Arkansas Press, Fayetteville)

The Israeli Information Center for Human Rights in the Occupied Territories (B'Tselem) (2019) "After a year of protests in Gaza: 11 military investigations", 1 charade (https://www.btselem.org/publications/summaries/201903_gaza_demonstrations_investigations_charade)

Tobonman, S. "Sabaaneh's social surrealism" in Sabaaneh, M, *White and Black: political cartoons from Palestine* (Charlottesville, Just World Publishers)

Tuqan, F. (1985) *A Mountainous Journey: A poet's autobiography* (Minnesota, Grey Wolf Press)

Tuqan, F. (2000) *Diwan Fadwa Tuqan* (Beirut, Dar al-Awdah)

Tzoreff, M. (2000) "Fadwa Tuqan's Autobiography: Restructuring a personal history into the Palestinian national narrative" in Shoshan, B. (ed) *Discourse on Gender/Gendered Discourse in the Middle East* (Praeger, Westpont, Conn.)

United Nations Office for the Coordination of Humanitarian Affairs (UNOCHA) (2018) "Over 700 road obstacles control Palestinian movement within the West Bank" *The Monthly Humanitarian Bulletin* (September 2018) https://www.ochaopt.org/content/over-700-road-obstacles-control-palestinian-movement-within-west-bank

Walker, T. and Gowers, A. (2003) *Arafat: The biography* (London, Virgin books)

Wright Mills, C. (1959) *The Sociological Imagination* (Oxford University Press)

Yeshurun, H. (2012) "Exile is so strong within me, I may bring it to the land" A landmark 1996 interview with Mahmoud Darwish *Journal of Palestine Studies* (Vol 42, No. 1) pp46-70

Yu, Liu Ze and Alhartani, N. A. K. (2018) "The image of women in the poetry of Mahmoud Darwish" *International Journal of Humanities, Philosophy and Language* Vol 1:3 (pp1-10)